The
Beekeepers

The
Beekeepers

How Humans Changed the
World of Bumble Bees

Dana L. Church

SCHOLASTIC
FOCUS
NEW YORK, NY

Library of Congress Cataloging-in-Publication Data

Names: Church, Dana L., author.
Title: The beekeepers : how humans changed the world of bumble bees / Dana L. Church,
PhD.
Description: First edition. | New York, NY : Scholastic Focus, 2021. | Includes bibliographi-
cal references and index. | Audience: Ages 8–12. | Identifiers: LCCN 2019054410 (print) |
LCCN 2019054411 (ebook) | ISBN 9781338565546 (hardback) | ISBN 9781338565553
(paperback) | ISBN 9781338565560 (ebk)
Subjects: LCSH: Bumblebees—Juvenile literature. | Bumblebees—Effect of human beings
on—Juvenile literature. | Pollination by bees—Juvenile literature. | Bee culture—Juvenile
literature.
Classification: LCC QL568.A6 C48 2021 (print) | LCC QL568.A6 (ebook) | DDC
595.79/9—dc23

1 2020

Printed in the U.S.A. 23
First edition, March 2021

Book design by Emily Muschinske

For my family

Table of Contents

The Bee Song

The following story and Traditional Knowledge were shared by Dr. Henry Lickers, an Elder of the Seneca Nation, Turtle Clan, Haudenosaunee (also known as the Iroquois).

The Haudenosaunee were the first agricultural peoples to live in what is now northeast Canada and the United States. They continue their agricultural practices today.

"I grew up on the Six Nation Reserve near Brantford, Ontario, Canada. I remember there was an old barn that they used to store hay bales in, for bedding for the cattle. One day I was in the barn and I saw a bumble bee fly out of one of the bales of hay. Then another, then another. Then I saw one fly back in. I watched them for a while as they flew in and out.

"I didn't know anything about bumble bees, but I was curious, so I grabbed a stick and approached the bale of hay. I used the stick to pry it apart little by little. Sure enough, didn't I come to a great group of [what looked like] . . . I want to call them gray, gray to white grapes, in a little bunch. The bees got a little upset, so I put the hay back and went to see my grandmother, who knew about these things.

"I told my grandmother what I saw, and she asked, 'Did you sing the bee song?' And I said, 'Grandma, I don't know the bee song.'

"'I will teach you the bee song,' she said.

"So, my grandmother followed me out to the barn. I noticed that as I approached the spot where I had seen the bumble bees, my grandmother stayed back. 'You go forward,' she instructed. 'And me as an adult will stay back. That is the proper way.'

"My grandmother told me to sit near the bees and wait and listen. I had to listen very carefully to how the wings of the bees were flapping. Sure enough, after a while I could hear it. It was like a humming sound. Some wings were flapping really, really fast, and others were flapping really, really low. Together, a type of harmony was created, or a chorus of notes. And as the bees worked, some were flapping their wings while others weren't. As I listened really carefully, I could hear what the song was. 'Now hum along,' said my grandmother. And as I hummed along, the bumble bees became very calm. 'Every bumble bee nest has its own song,' explained my grandmother. 'You have to listen for it.'

"As I hummed along with the bees, it was as if to them I

wasn't even there. Or, it was as if I was another bee. I started to slowly take the nest apart, being careful not to just rip it apart. You have to take a really slow time to look. 'You'll see these things that are about the size of a big pea,' my grandmother said. 'When you see those, don't reach in and grab them all. You grab just one. The bees might start flying around a little bit more, but you keep the humming going. The bees are a peaceful tribe. The bee makes that honey for her own kids, and makes it for *any* kids. But unless you treat it with respect and hum to them, they won't give it up easily.'

"'You put that little pill in your mouth,' my grandmother continued, 'hold it, and put the nest back together again. Then you can back away, squash the pill in your mouth, and eat the whole thing.'

"As I backed away from the nest, I squashed the 'pill' in my mouth with my tongue. It felt like . . . I want to say it's like a gelatin coat. You know, how Jell-O goes when it gets hard? It's like that. And of course, when I squashed it, the honey came out. But my grandmother never called it honey, though. She called it something else, like a honeydew, or a dew type of thing. She said that it's sweet, like maple sap, but not overly sweet like honey bee honey. And as I tasted it, I realized she was right.

"After that day I found a number of bumble bee nests. They really interested me. There would have been about three or four acres of bush and trees, and I usually found them around the edge, where you had thick grass. I found them in there. And there was usually some type of structure with it, like a rock. So, they would be beside the rock but in the grass, and you could see how they were sort of pulling the grass down to it. I remember one nest was at the edge of a marsh, in an old muskrat house. But I never told anyone where I found the bee nests. I kept it a secret. And I always left fresh grass very near to the nest for the bumble bees.

"My grandmother told me other things about bumble bees, too. She said that bumble bees were one of the few animals that when they started out, they had no fur, no clothes on them. And so, they got cold. The Creator said, 'Well, we can't have that.' But the bumble bees didn't want just one set of clothes! They asked the Creator for many different sets. So, when you see a bumble bee going into the ground, she's going in actually to change her clothes. She changes her clothes so she can look pretty. And if you watch the bees carefully, like I did, you'll see they groom themselves. They groom themselves and when their clothes get too dirty, they just go in and change them! And their nests are porous. Even the underground stuff. And my grandmother said that was so the dew and the mist can get into their nest and clean their clothes for them.

"And so, to us as Native People, the bumble bees were all

one family. All they did was change their clothes every once in a while, to confuse everybody.

"My people were farmers, so we needed pollinators. Bumble bees are very important to us. Sometimes bumble bees are confused with honey bees, but honey bees are not *native* to North America. That means they are not naturally from there. They were introduced by Europeans. Bumble bees are native, though, and they are very important for the Three Sisters. There was a tall sister, who was very tall. She was the corn. There was another sister who was not so tall, but she was clingy. That's the beans. And then there was a short, fat sister. Of course, that's the squash. Corn, beans, and squash. They were planted together and so they grow together as the Three Sisters.

"Our fields were vast: two, three, four, five hundred acres of land. And the tradition goes that you plant the Three Sisters in circles with a common center that will all ripen at different times. Each circle is farther from the village. And the last circle is the circle that you leave for the animals. So, the deer and the raccoons and all those will come and eat of that last circle around your field.

"So, anything that helps you get a better crop were considered your helpers. Bumble bees were like, wow, they were good people!"

CHAPTER ONE

New Bees on the Block

Millions of years ago, before the first humans appeared on the planet, bumble bees buzzed from flower to flower. The earliest bumble bee fossil records we have date back to what we call the Oligocene era (34 million to 23 million years ago), millions of years after the dinosaurs roamed the Earth (see Figure 1-1).

We haven't actually found a whole lot of bumble bee fossils. But evidence from the few that we have,

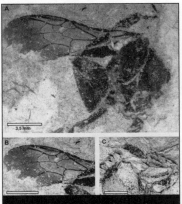

FIGURE 1-1. A fossil of *Bombus cerdanyensis*, approximately 23 million to 5 million years old, found in Spain.

combined with clues from bumble bees that exist today, led scientists to believe that bumble bees probably originally came from somewhere in Asia. They then traveled west through Europe and North America, and finally headed south to South America (see Figure 1-2).

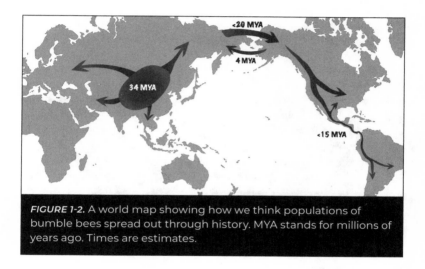

FIGURE 1-2. A world map showing how we think populations of bumble bees spread out through history. MYA stands for millions of years ago. Times are estimates.

Today, bumble bees still live on those same continents. Thanks to their big size and fur-covered bodies, they are well adapted to cooler climates. So, they are naturally found in mild, mountainous, and arctic zones. However, a few species can also be found in more tropical areas in Southeast Asia and Central and South America. Figure 1-3 shows where you can find naturally occurring species of bumble bees around the world.

Once humans came along—specifically, traveling,

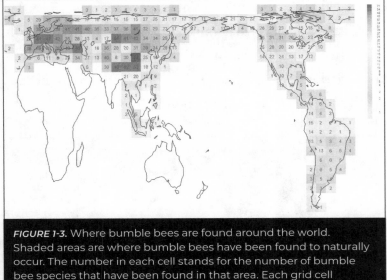

FIGURE 1-3. Where bumble bees are found around the world. Shaded areas are where bumble bees have been found to naturally occur. The number in each cell stands for the number of bumble bee species that have been found in that area. Each grid cell represents an equal area, about 235,908 mi². Darker areas have a greater number of bumble bee species, and lighter areas have fewer bumble bee species. One part of China has the most, with seventy-one.

continent-hopping humans—the spread of bumble bees around the world started to look a bit different. Thanks to human influence, there are now species of bumble bees in places where these species have never been before. And probably never would have been, if it wasn't for our helping hands.

BUMBLE BEES IN ICELAND

A hulking Viking ship sliced through the ocean waves. It was a cargo ship, on a long and treacherous journey to a destination we now know as Iceland. The trip would take months. The ship's storage area was filled to bursting with food and supplies. Tucked deep within one of the many bales of hay, which would eventually be used to feed livestock in the new land, was a tiny, fuzzy, slumbering queen bumble bee.

This bumble bee had fluffy yellow-black-yellow bands down her body, ending in a tuft of white fur on her rear end. Centuries later, this species of bumble bee would be called the heath bumble bee (*Bombus jonellus*).

How did the queen survive the months-long voyage? Bumble bees need food to eat, which for them means the sugary liquid called nectar that is found in flowers.

FIGURE 1-4. The heath bumble bee (*Bombus jonellus*).

There were certainly no flowers aboard the Viking ship! Luckily enough for the queen, the ship was traveling at a time of the year when she would normally be in hibernation: the sleeplike state some animals go into during the winter months. So, she just slept the trip away. And little did this queen know, when she woke up, she would be the first of her species to arrive in Iceland.

The earliest Icelandic reference to what were probably

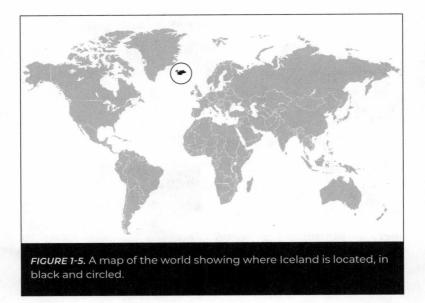

FIGURE 1-5. A map of the world showing where Iceland is located, in black and circled.

bumble bees is dated at about 1640: Writing from that period uses the word *hunangsflugur*, or honeyflies, which is the traditional Icelandic name for bumble bees. Today it is believed that bumble bees arrived in Iceland by "hitch-hiking" on Viking ships, just like the queen bumble bee described earlier. However, there is the possibility that someone back in the days of the Vikings intentionally hid that queen bumble bee among the cargo in order to introduce it to the new land. If they did, they kept poor records of their actions, or they made no records at all.

Whether the introduction of bumble bees to Iceland was intentional or not, human actions around the world have impacted where various species of bumble bees are found. Today there are many more different species of bumble bees in Iceland besides the heath. For instance, there is the tree bumble bee (*Bombus hypnorum*), which, instead of having black-and-yellow fur like many bumble bee species, has a reddish-brown thorax (the bee's middle section behind the head, where the legs and wings are attached), a black abdomen (the last, larger section of the body behind the thorax), and a white tail.

FIGURE 1-6. The tree bumble bee (*Bombus hypnorum*).

The white-tailed bumble bee (*Bombus lucorum*) has the more typical black-and-yellow coloring, with a lemon-yellow "collar" near the top of the thorax and another yellow band across the abdomen.

FIGURE 1-7. White-tailed bumble bee (*Bombus lucorum*). This bumble bee has large balls of pollen on her back legs.

Like the heath and tree bumble bees, it, too, has a white rear end, hence its name. Funnily enough, these

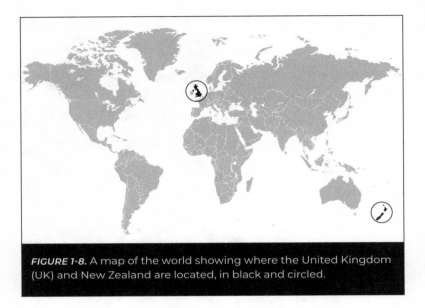

FIGURE 1-8. A map of the world showing where the United Kingdom (UK) and New Zealand are located, in black and circled.

and other species of bumble bees in Iceland were often first discovered near shipping ports or airports. Stowaways on human travel, perhaps?

BUMBLE BEES IN NEW ZEALAND

Now let's jump to the late 1800s. A steamship glides across the ocean heading from the United Kingdom to New Zealand. On board is a peculiar type of passenger: bumble bees.

Unlike the case in Iceland where bumble bees were likely furry little stowaways that happened to hide among the cargo, people intentionally imported these bumble bees from their native UK to New Zealand to pollinate a plant called red clover.

At the time, red clover was a hot commodity. People used horses for transportation and working farmland, and these horses needed to eat. Cattle and sheep needed to eat as well. So red clover—which did not naturally grow in New Zealand but is fantastic feed for certain farm animals—was imported from the UK. Folks in New Zealand quickly realized that the red clover was not growing on its own; seeds needed constant planting, and continuously importing red clover seed was expensive. Someone realized what was needed was something to pollinate the red clover. Enter bumble bees.

Bumble bees were excellent candidates to pollinate New Zealand's red clover fields. For one thing, they often buzzed around red clover in the UK. Their furry bodies and their ability to control their internal temperature allowed them to keep warm and forage (collect food) during cloudy, chilly days when other bees or insects would be hiding. Also, red clover is tricky for most pollinators[1] to handle: It requires heavier insects to get at the pollen, and the nectar tubes of the flower are quite long, such that insects with short tongues can't reach the sugary liquid. Clover-loving, furry, warm, heavy, and longer-tongued . . . bumble bees were the winner!

---

1. A *pollinator* is an animal that moves pollen from one flower to another, allowing the plant to reproduce. Bumble bees are pollinators, along with other bees (such as honey bees), butterflies, moths, beetles, flies, bats, and certain types of birds.

Things weren't so easy at first. A couple of bumble bee nests were dug up (bumble bees often like to make their homes in old, underground rodent nests), and placed on a ship. But by the time the ship made it from the UK to New Zealand (a journey that took at least a month), all the bumble bees were dead.

How could they keep bumble bees alive on a steamship for a month or more? Someone noticed that queen bumble bees hibernate underground during winter. In spring, when the temperature warms, the queens dig themselves out, find a place to make a nest, and start laying eggs. What if the bumble bee queens traveled on the ship when they usually hibernated and were kept cool to fool them into thinking it was winter? That way, when the ship arrived in New Zealand, the queens could be warmed up, they could emerge from hibernation, and they would be ready to start their little families. Plus, just like that first bumble bee traveling to Iceland, the ship's crew didn't have to worry about feeding them during the journey if the bumble bee queens were in hibernation.

So, a reward was offered to anyone who could dig up a plump, hibernating queen bumble bee. The crew collected over two hundred queens! These queens that were shipped to New Zealand were in one of the first ships that was built with a refrigeration unit, so they likely shared the trip with frozen meats and other cargo. Not all of the bumble bee queens survived, but a fair number of them did, and they were released on New Zealand's South Island. This venture was declared a success, and it was repeated shortly after that with another two hundred or so queen bumble bees. Again, not all of the queens survived, but a number of them did manage to fly off into their new New Zealand turf.

FIGURE 1-9. The ruderal bumble bee (*Bombus ruderatus*).

The folks involved in this bumble bee importation operation forgot to do one important thing, however: write down what kinds of bumble bees and how many they released!

Today we know that four bumble bee species live in New Zealand: the garden bumble bee (*Bombus hortorum*), the buff-tailed bumble bee (*Bombus terrestris*), the short-haired bumble bee (*Bombus subterraneus*), and the ruderal bumble bee (*Bombus ruderatus*).[2] So at least these four species of bumble bee were likely aboard the ships. The buff-tailed and ruderal bumble bees have done particularly well:

2.　You might have noticed that some types of bumble bee species look very similar, such as the buff-tailed bumble bee and the white-tailed bumble bee. Sometimes even scientists have a hard time telling them apart! More about this will come in Chapter Two.

They are now found throughout large areas of New Zealand's South Island.

BUMBLE BEES IN CHILE

By as recently as the early 1980s, humans were still influencing where bumble bees could be found throughout the world. Let's travel to Chile. Red clover was still in demand, and Chile has a lot of it. The funny thing is that Chile has no native bees that are particularly good at pollinating red clover. Red clover was brought into South America, so there were no natural pollinators for it. Honey bees and some solitary bees were seen feeding

FIGURE 1-10. The buff-tailed bumble bee (*Bombus terrestris*).

FIGURE 1-11. Map of South America. The country of Chile is found along the lower left-hand side of the continent.

from the clover, but they didn't make much of an impact. (We'll learn more about honey bees and solitary bees in

Chapter Two.) Chilean folks looked around and saw the success places such as the UK and New Zealand were having with long-tongued bumble bees. So, Chile decided to import a few ruderal bumble bee queens from New Zealand.

Why bring in bumble bees from New Zealand? There were a couple of reasons. One reason was that Chile and New Zealand are both in the Southern Hemisphere. This means that the life cycle of queen bumble bees from both places are timed such that the queens are flying out and about at the same time that many of the flowers in Chile are in bloom. The queen bumble bees could, therefore, be released directly into their new Chilean home and not have to wait for flowers to blossom in order to get nectar and pollen for food. Another reason was that queen bumble bees from New Zealand did not seem to have any of the diseases or parasites[3] that are found in bumble bees in Europe and America, so they would be less likely to make other bumble bees in Chile sick.

And why import ruderal bumble bee queens versus the other species of bumble bees that were in New Zealand? This particular species was chosen because they are laidback compared to others (that is, they are less likely to become aggressive and sting), and at the time they were the

---

3.　A *parasite* is a creature that lives on or inside an animal, feeding off that animal, and causing the animal harm.

most common long-tongued bumble bee in New Zealand. Also, unlike the other New Zealand bumble bee species, ruderal bumble bees often nested in areas with few trees, which is the kind of area where red clover grows.

So, in 1982, a couple of scientists collected 199 ruderal bumble bee queens from New Zealand and shipped them to Chile. Compared to the queens that initially traveled to New Zealand in the 1800s, these queens got first-class treatment. For one thing, the trip was a whole lot shorter: seven to ten days of travel compared to more than a month. Each queen had her own tiny screened cage with a plastic bottle cap filled with a sugar water solution (to mimic flower nectar) that was refilled every twenty-four hours. An unlimited, all-you-can-eat buffet! The temperature also stayed on the chilly side to keep the bees calm. (The colder it gets, the less bees move. If it is chilly enough, the bees go into a sort of deep-sleep state called torpor.)

Upon arrival in Chile, the 145 out of 199 ruderal bumble bee queens that survived the trip were released at a site with red clover. The process was repeated a year later in 1983: This time 192 ruderal bumble bee queens were collected, shipped, and 169 of them survived and were released into their new, red-clover-filled home.

A few months later, the scientists returned to the release sites in Chile and found ruderal worker bees, with their yellow-black-yellow thorax, a yellow band on the abdomen where it meets the thorax, and a white tail. That meant at least some of the queens managed to lay eggs in their new Chilean home and establish their colonies of workers, who would then go on to pollinate the red clover. Success!

Not only did ruderal bumble bees end up pollinating Chilean red clover, but their population began to spread. They even crossed the Andes Mountains and settled into Argentina!

But ruderal bumble bees are not the only type of bumble bee that has been brought into Chile. Chileans have imported buff-tailed bumble bees into their country for years. As we will see in later chapters, the population of buff-tailed bumble bees has exploded across Chile and Argentina, putting a native species of bumble bee at great risk of extinction. In fact, the buff-tailed bumble bee is quite a world traveler! This bee has even made its way into Tasmania.

BUMBLE BEES IN TASMANIA

On a bright summer's day in February 1992, a gentleman by the name of Frank King was strolling through a garden in a place called Battery Point in Tasmania. Tasmania is a state of the country of Australia; it's a triangular island located about 150 miles south of the mainland. The timing of the seasons in Australia is the opposite to that of northern countries, with summer weather in the months of December, January, and February. And since the winter months of June, July, and August do not get anywhere near as cold as northern countries such as Canada and the northern United States, it is possible for flowers to bloom in Tasmania year-round.

On his stroll, King likely saw a number of native bees buzzing about the garden. These bees would have been quite small, some as small as a grain of rice. They wouldn't have been very colorful, and they wouldn't have been very furry. Then King spotted something striking: a huge, fuzzy black-and-yellow bumble bee. He had probably never seen a bumble bee before, since bumble bees are not originally from Australia. He managed to capture two of them, and he brought them to the Tasmanian Museum and Art Gallery in the nearby city of Hobart to show the experts there. These bumble bees were identified as buff-tailed bumble bees, the same species that is found in the UK— about 10,500 miles away! How did these bumble bees get all the way to Tasmania? There was no way they could have made such a long journey without help!

It just so happens that New Zealand is about 1,500 miles to the east of Tasmania. You'll remember that bumble bees were introduced to New Zealand from the UK in the 1800s. By the 1990s, they were very much established in their newfound New Zealand home. So, it is likely that the bumble bees that King spotted came from New Zealand. But 1,500 miles is still too far for a bumble bee to fly, especially across a cold ocean! Did they hitchhike on a ship, like the bumble bees that traveled to Iceland? After all, King saw the bumble bees not far from shipping docks. Or perhaps someone intentionally brought them there?

It's likely that someone brought them to Tasmania on purpose. As we will see in later chapters, in the late 1980s and early 1990s, someone discovered that bumble bees are superstar pollinators when it comes to greenhouse tomatoes. And tomatoes are a big business. Walk through any grocery store and you'll see pasta sauce, tomato juice, tomato paste, pizza sauce, canned tomatoes, ketchup, salsa, and a wide variety of frozen or pre-prepared pizzas, pastas, and other meals that contain some form of tomatoes.

When news spread that bumble bees can help produce bigger, tastier tomatoes, people started bumble bee breeding programs. Commercial bumble bee companies began popping up and shipping bumble bees to tomato farmers around the world. Well, except for Australia. Australia has very strict laws against bringing in foreign species. Bumble bees were not allowed. And Australia has no bumble bee species of its own. So, Australian tomato farmers were missing out. Was it just a coincidence that bumble bees started showing up in Tasmania around the time of the bumble bee boom? We may never know.

In 1996, just four years after King first saw buff-tailed bumble bees, this species was seen about twenty-four miles north of where it was first spotted, as well as about thirty-seven miles south. They seemed to be spreading across the island at about seven to eight miles per year. They were seen mostly in cities, but they were also sighted in the mountains and a national park.

To get a better handle on just how well buff-tailed bumble bees were making a home in Tasmania, in 1999 a team of two scientists from the UK, Dr. Jane Stout and Dr. Dave Goulson, traveled to the island and took an extensive road trip. They drove around the state, stopping whenever they spotted a patch of flowers. They would look for bumble bees, and if they spotted some, they marked the location on a map.[4] Soon they discovered they could easily find bumble bees in people's gardens. And Tasmanians keep lovely gardens, thanks to the relatively nice weather year-round! So, Dr. Stout and Dr. Goulson knocked on people's doors and asked if they could look for bees in their yards. And because bumble bees were easy to spot compared to the smaller native and less furry bee species in Tasmania, often the

---

4.   One tricky aspect of this type of research is that if they didn't see any bumble bees, they couldn't be sure if there were actually none in that area, or if it was because they were unlucky, and didn't happen to see any at that time.

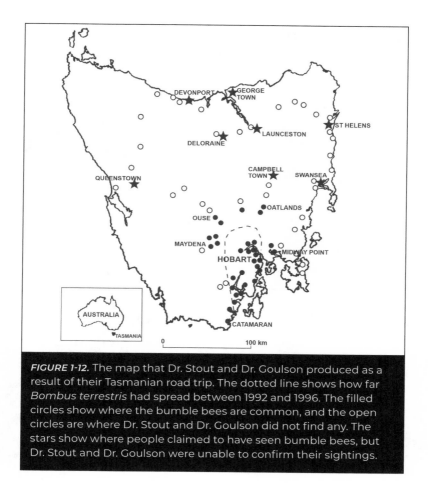

FIGURE 1-12. The map that Dr. Stout and Dr. Goulson produced as a result of their Tasmanian road trip. The dotted line shows how far *Bombus terrestris* had spread between 1992 and 1996. The filled circles show where the bumble bees are common, and the open circles are where Dr. Stout and Dr. Goulson did not find any. The stars show where people claimed to have seen bumble bees, but Dr. Stout and Dr. Goulson were unable to confirm their sightings.

homeowners would tell tales of seeing bumble bees themselves. Eventually Dr. Stout and Dr. Goulson produced a map that gives an idea of how much buff-tailed bumble bees had spread over the years (see Figure 1-12).

Looking at Dr. Stout and Dr. Goulson's map, based on unconfirmed sightings, it seems as though these bees were spreading across the island. The species was also spreading north. Would they eventually land in mainland Australia and establish populations there? First, they would have to cross the 150-mile divide that separates Tasmania from the mainland. Past research found that bumble bees can fly about nine to nineteen miles over water. So, they couldn't fly the whole distance. However, there are a number of little islands along the way, so in theory bumble bees could reach mainland Australia by island-hopping. Like a cruise for pollinators!

There had been attempts to introduce bumble bees to mainland Australia back in the late 1800s and early 1900s (before strict Australian import laws existed), but they were unsuccessful. One report suggests that predatory Australian birds were to blame. Or, perhaps the newly arrived bumble bees could not find nesting sites, or they couldn't adapt to the warmer climate. If bumble bees ended up island-hopping from Tasmania to the mainland, they would have some challenges to overcome.

Not a lot of details exist about these early introductions to mainland Australia, including which species of bumble bees were released. Was it the buff-tailed bumble bee, or another species? The buff-tailed is known to be pretty hardy and can adapt to new locations quite well. Could this include mainland Australia? Only time would tell.

SOUNDING THE ALARM

Since bumble bees were introduced to Iceland, New Zealand, Chile, and Tasmania, these buzzing teddy bears of the insect world have spread well beyond their original sites of release. And, for the most part, in terms of red clover and greenhouse tomatoes, they have been busy pollinating crops as intended.

So there hasn't been any harm in humans transporting bumble bees to new habitats . . . or has there?

Some scientists are now quite concerned about possible negative consequences of introducing bumble bees to areas far beyond where they are originally found. If you plunk bumble bees down into an area of flowering plants in a foreign land, chances are there are already creatures that depend on those plants for food. A number of different animals collect pollen and nectar from flowers: birds, bats, mammals, and other insects. Plus, bumble bees make up a small number of the twenty-five thousand known species of bee. The new bumble bees would have what is called a niche overlap with the native pollinators. Niche overlap happens when two or more species of plants or animals share the same food, living space, predators, and other things in their day-to-day living. The big question is: Is there enough food and living space for everyone?

Because new bumble bees might have a niche overlap with other animals does not necessarily mean that they compete for nectar and pollen with those animals. You might think there are enough flowers to go around.

It's difficult for us to figure out whether foreign bumble bees are actually competing with native wildlife. However, scientists know of several bumble bee characteristics that might give them a competitive edge. For one thing, compared to other bee species, bumble bees begin foraging earlier in the morning when the temperature is cooler, thanks to their larger size and hairy body. Bumble bees, therefore, get first dibs on flowers' nectar stores, which, depending on the type of flower, may take a while to refill. Bumble bees also tend to fly farther distances when foraging compared to other bees: Some species of bumble bees fly at least two and a half miles from their nest site to find food, whereas other types of bees don't fly as far. And being a social species of bee might be an advantage: There is evidence that when a worker bumble bee returns to her nest after a foraging trip, the scent of the nectar she carries is a hint to other worker bumble bees in the colony as to where to find good food. She also may give off a unique scent that encourages other worker bumble bees to leave the nest to forage. This means that bumble bees may locate nectar and pollen resources more quickly, compared to solitary species of bee (most species of bee are solitary), which need to find nectar and pollen by themselves on a trial and error basis.

Besides potentially creating competition with native

pollinating animals, some scientists also think imported bumble bees might carry unwanted passengers. One type of potential passenger is parasites. Others could be microscopic, disease-causing creatures called pathogens. These pathogens and parasites might come from other places and infect native species. For instance, bumble bees in New Zealand carry a parasitic nematode (a worm-like creature) and three mite species (which are tiny, parasitic arachnids), and these are all thought to have come from the UK. The tricky thing about parasites and pathogens is that you often can't tell with the naked eye whether a single bumble bee or a whole colony of bumble bees is infected. Parasites and pathogens tend to exist inside the bee's gut or in their feces (poop). So how would you check to see if the bumble bees you want to import are completely healthy? Unfortunately, we haven't completely figured that out yet.

Newly introduced bumble bees might start pollinating weeds, too. These weeds would then multiply and might choke out other, more desirable plants. The increase in weeds could affect the native pollinators of the choked-out plants by leaving them less food. The native pollinators starve and become more susceptible to disease because of lower nutrition.

It is a tangled web that importing bumble bees may weave. As you will see in the following chapters, the introduction of bumble bees to Iceland, New Zealand, Chile, and Tasmania was only the tip of the iceberg.

CHAPTER TWO

Humble-Bees

What Are Bumble Bees, Anyway?

Since the first little stowaway on a Viking ship, humans have learned a lot about bumble bees and what makes them different from other types of bees.

Bumble bees, like all other types of bees, are invertebrates, which means they have no backbone or spine. They are also insects, which means they breathe air, have six legs, their body is covered in an exoskeleton (a hard shell), and they have three body parts, which we went over in the last chapter: a head, a thorax, and an abdomen.

The head of a bumble bee includes the eyes, mouthparts, and antennae. Bumble bees, and other bees, actually have five eyes: two large compound eyes and three small ocelli.

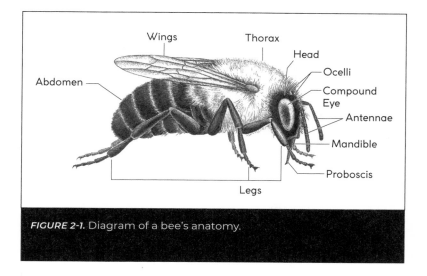

FIGURE 2-1. Diagram of a bee's anatomy.

The ocelli are found between the two compound eyes and are arranged in a triangle. The ocelli are used to detect light intensity and perhaps help the bee know how its body is positioned in relation to the space around it; they cannot focus or make images. Making images is the function of the compound eyes. Each compound eye is made up of thousands of individual hexagon-shaped lenses called facets. Not only do the compound eyes allow the bee to see, but tiny hairs where the facets touch one another allow the bee to detect airflow when it flies, helping it to navigate.

The mouthparts of a bumble bee consist of the mandibles and proboscis. The mandibles are the jaws of the bee:

They are spoon-shaped and strong, and are used for eating pollen, cutting and shaping wax in the nest, grooming, feeding larvae (baby bees that look like little white worms), and dragging dead bees and debris out of the nest. The proboscis is the bee's tongue. When the bee is not using it, it is folded up into a space beneath the bee's mouth. When it is extended, the bee uses it to suck up nectar from flowers like drinking liquid from a straw. The length of the proboscis differs between different species of bumble bees: Some species, such as the buff-tailed bumble bee, have a rather short proboscis, whereas the proboscis of the garden bumble bee is almost the same length as its body! Finally, a bee's antennae allow it the sense of smell.

A bumble bee's thorax includes its wings, wing muscles, and legs. On each of the two hind legs of bumble bees (and other pollen-collecting bees, such as honey bees), there is a smooth and slightly spoon-shaped section called the pollen basket or corbicula. When a bee collects nectar from flowers, she often becomes dusted with grains of pollen. Before leaving the flower, she uses her front and middle sets of legs to smooth the grains down toward her back legs, and packs the pollen grains into balls on her corbiculae. This allows her to carry the pollen back to the nest. Bumble bees, and other pollen-collecting bees, can often be seen flying with blobs of pollen on their back legs. Pollen can be a range of colors, from yellow to white to orange to purple.

The abdomen of a bumble bee contains the digestive and reproductive organs and the stinger. The bumble bee's honey stomach, or crop, is an expandable bag that, when full of nectar, takes up most of the space in the bee's abdomen. Bumble bees do have intestines and a rectum, and when they poop, it is a sticky, brownish-yellow liquid.[1]

As an insect, bumble bees don't have lungs like humans; they breathe using holes called spiracles that are found along the side of their body. The spiracles are attached to tubes inside the insect called trachea that deliver air to the insect's cells. And, like other insects, bumble bees don't have a circulatory system like ours, with veins and arteries. Instead, their yellow-colored blood, called hemolymph, just kind of sloshes around inside their bodies. Bees do have a heart, but it looks like a tube that runs along the inside top of their abdomen, above their stomach and other organs.

The brain of a bee is about the size of a sesame seed. It is made up of about one million brain cells, called neurons. A human brain contains around eighty-five billion neurons, but this doesn't mean that a bee's brain is not complex: Each one of its neurons can branch off in so many directions it looks as complicated as a fully grown tree. And a bee's brain

---

1.   During my years studying bumble bees, I had many a bee poop on me. It's actually not so bad.

can have about one billion synapses, which are the connections between neurons. (As a comparison, a human brain has trillions and trillions of synapses.) Along the inside of the bee's body and connected to the brain are several nerve centers, called ganglia, that help control different parts of the bee's body. Even if a bee loses its head, it can still beat its wings, move its legs, and sting!

What makes bumble bees different from other bees? Most obvious is their size and fur. Bumble bees are generally larger and much hairier than other bees. As we saw in the previous chapter, there are a number of different types, or species, of bumble bees. A *species* means a group of animals or plants with similar features (for example, fur-color pattern) that can breed with each other. Each bumble bee species has its own distinctive fur pattern. For instance, the giant *Bombus dahlbomii* has a body covered in rusty-colored fur,[2] whereas the buff-tailed bumble bee has the more familiar black-and-yellow coloring, ending with a white rear. Over 250 species of bumble bees have been identified all over the world! That's a lot of different bumble bee fur patterns. In fact, scientists have found that bumble bee fur colors and patterns can vary *within* some species as well. Sometimes it's difficult for

---

2.   In Argentina, *Bombus dahlbomii* is called *Manganga*, and in Chile it is called *Moscardón*. Because of its large size it has been described as a flying mouse. To account for its size and brightly colored fur, in this book we'll refer to it as the giant ginger bumble bee.

bumble bee experts to tell the different species of bumble bees apart. When this happens, DNA testing is the sure way to identify a species. Similar to how each person has their own unique fingerprint, each bumble bee species has its own pattern of DNA (deoxyribonucleic acid). DNA is found in cells, and they are like microscopic beads on a string that contain the instructions or recipe for how to build the organism. To do a DNA test for a bumble bee, scientists take a tiny piece of a bumble bee's tarsus (foot), and use special equipment to look at the DNA pattern. This is also called genetic testing.

In all, there are over four hundred different bumble bee color patterns: various combinations of black, white, yellows, oranges, and reds that occur over different parts of the bumble bees' bodies. What's really cool is that certain color patterns tend to cluster in different parts of the world. The darkest bumble bees are usually found in the tropics. The palest bumble bees are mostly in the intermediate northern latitudes, such as in the United States, Canada, and the United Kingdom, where their colors are thought to blend in with grasslands. And finally, the more strongly banded bumble bees are more widespread in parts of the world where bumble bees are found.

Although 250 species of bumble bees might seem like a lot, this is only a sliver of the 20,000 species of bees that have been identified around the world. Most of the 20,000 bee species are known as solitary bees.

After a female solitary bee mates, she makes her own nest, which includes about ten individual "cells," called brood cells. She then stocks each cell with food (pollen and nectar), lays an egg in each cell (each egg is about the size, shape, and color of a grain of white rice), and dies. She doesn't see her eggs hatch into new bees. There are no queen solitary bees and no worker bees; just male or female bees hatch from the eggs. They fly off to find food for themselves, mate, and then the cycle starts over again.

Where a solitary bee builds its nest depends on its species. Most solitary bees choose to build their nest underground, burrowing tunnels in bare, dry, light soil, or they use nests that were made previously by ants, wasps, or other solitary bees. Some species of solitary bees build their nests out of mud, chew holes into wooden structures, or use pre-existing holes in trees and other objects.[3] A solitary bee nest can be found all on its own, isolated from other nests, or a nest can be found among a group of nests of other solitary bees.[4] But the female owners of these nests do not help each other in nest building and other chores. Each bee keeps to herself (hence the name *solitary* bees).

---

3.   The "bee houses" that have lots of tiny holes for bees and are advertised on the internet and sold in stores usually cater to solitary bees.

4.   One cluster of solitary bee nests occupied 3,875,000 square feet (about seventy football fields) and extended about 4.35 miles (the length of thirty Golden Gate Bridges) along a bank of the Barysh River in the former USSR. There were an estimated twelve million nests!

Bumble bees operate quite differently. As opposed to solitary bees, bumble bees are considered social bees. This means they live in a colony made up of many other bees, and all the bees cooperate to keep things running smoothly. This includes making sure there is enough food stored in the nest for everyone, that the eggs and larvae are fed and kept warm, and that the temperature in the nest stays steady.

Bumble bee colonies have a life cycle that is a bit different from the life cycle of solitary bees as well. At the end of summer, after a queen bumble bee mates, she digs a tunnel underground and sleeps for the winter in a state of torpor. When spring comes, the queen digs her way out and starts to look for a nest. If you see a big, fat bumble bee in spring and she's flying low to the ground in a zigzag motion, chances are it is a queen bumble bee looking for a home. As mentioned in Chapter One, bumble bee queens tend to make their nests underground, often in old mouse or vole nests.

Once the queen has found a nest, she begins to lay eggs. Like the eggs of solitary bees, each egg is about the size, shape, and color of a grain of white rice. The queen covers each egg in wax that she squeezes out of her abdomen. (When the wax first comes out it looks like flakes of dandruff.) The eggs will hatch into larvae. Each larva spins a cocoon around itself and it is inside this cocoon that the larva grows into a bee. In bumble bee colonies, all of the larvae that develop in the spring and most of the summer become female worker bees. Near the end of summer, the larvae develop into new queens and male bees.

After laying her first cluster of eggs, the queen bumble bee leaves her nest from time to time to find food for herself and the larvae. It is important that the larvae get pollen, as it contains protein, a nutrient that they need to grow into adult bumble bees. The queen may also form a nectar pot out of wax where she can store extra nectar for herself.

Once the eggs hatch into larvae, they grow into female worker bees. The queen then stays in the nest while the worker bees take over the task of leaving the nest to find pollen and nectar. The queen continues to lay more and more eggs that will hatch and grow into more and more worker bees.[5] Each worker bee lives for several weeks.

When worker bees are not outside the nest finding pollen and nectar, they help out with other "housekeeping" tasks. They can be sitting on the eggs and larvae to keep them warm and buzzing their wings to keep the nest temperature steady. There are even "undertaker bees" that carry dead bumble bees from the nest and dump them outside. Dumping them outside not only keeps the nest clean, but it also provides food for animals that eat bees. If the dead bee is

---

5.   I've seen many baby bumble bees chew their way out of their cocoons, and they are quite cute! When they first hatch, their fur is gray and silky. After a day or two the fur turns the color of the bee's species.

not eaten, its body breaks down and provides nourishment for the soil.

Around late summer, the eggs that the queen bumble bee lays hatch into new queens and male bumble bees. Once these larvae are grown, the queens and males leave the nest to find a mate. Male bumble bees die after mating. But after a queen mates, she digs a hole into the ground where she will hibernate for the winter. Then the cycle begins again in spring when she digs her way out.

Out of the twenty thousand bee species on Earth, the species that most people are familiar with is *Apis mellifera*: the domestic honey bee. As their name implies, honey bees are the bees that make honey—and lots of it. They are also the bees that beekeepers keep in wooden boxes. These boxes are quite big because there are thousands of bees in a honey bee colony. A colony of bumble bees, on the other hand, usually just has several hundred bees. Because bumble bee colonies are much smaller, and they don't need to store honey for the winter like honey bees do (more on that momentarily), they don't keep as much nectar in the nest. They usually just save enough nectar to tide them over for a few days of bad weather. So, it's not worthwhile for humans to try to harvest the honey from bumble bee nests.

Although bees are well known for their black-and-yellow coloring, honey bees are more light brown in color.

They are also much smaller and thinner than bumble bees.

In winter, while bumble bee queens slumber underground, honey bee queens rest in their hives, surrounded by their thousands of worker bees, who form a tight cluster around her. The worker honey bees keep the queen warm by shivering their flight muscles. Throughout the winter all the honey bees eat the honey that is stored in the hexagon-shaped combs of the hive. As spring approaches, the worker bees begin to feed the queen a thick white liquid from glands near their mandibles. This is called royal jelly, and it provides the queen with the protein she needs to start laying eggs. The queen honey bee then starts laying eggs in the cells that have been kept warm in the hive. After the larvae hatch from the eggs, the worker honey bees feed them royal jelly, but after about three days, the larvae begin eating honey and pollen exclusively and develop into new worker bees.

When spring arrives, the queen continues to lay eggs, and more and more worker honey bees emerge. Soon there is not enough room in the hive, and the worker bees start preparing for what is called a swarm. To prepare, they feed several larvae royal jelly exclusively: A larva that is fed only royal jelly develops into a queen honey bee. The original queen bee and about half of the worker bees begin to gorge themselves with honey. Then, once these bees are stuffed, they leave the hive in a swirling mass and form a cluster on a nearby tree branch. While the honey bees hang out there, several honey bees act as "scout bees," flying off in search of a new shelter. After they find a suitable place, they report back to the swarm, and the cluster of honey bees leave their branch to set up their new home.

Back at the original hive, the new queen honey bees hatch. If there are enough worker honey bees left, one of these queens may lead another swarm, called the after-swarm. Some honey bee colonies may produce as many as four afterswarms. After the last afterswarm leaves the hive, the remaining new queen honey bees hatch and fight to the death, stinging each other, until only one remains. This queen then flies off to mate, and once she has mated, returns to the hive. By this time of year, it is time for the hive to focus on storing as much pollen and nectar as possible, in preparation for winter. Throughout this swarm and after-swarm period, some larvae have developed into male honey bees, called drones. Any drones that have not left the hive in search of a queen are now kicked out of the hive by the worker bees.[6] Once the cold days of winter arrive, the worker honey bees cluster around the queen to keep her warm, and the cycle continues.

---

6.   Like male bumble bees, drones, except for their role in mating, are pretty much useless. They don't help with any of the hive or colony tasks, and just hang around, eating up the honey and nectar collected by female worker bees.

Besides swarming behavior and making lots of honey, honey bees are also well known for their "dancing." When a worker honey bee finds a good flower patch, she returns to the hive and "tells" her other sister bees about it by performing specific movements, so that they, too, can go out into the world and find the bounty. She will scuttle forward in a straight line for an inch or so, then circle to the left, scuttle in another straight line, then circle to the right, forming a figure eight. Humans have spent a lot of time attempting to decode this dance language, and we've discovered a few things. For example, the length of the straight run tells other bees the distance to the flower patch, with roughly one second of scuttling equaling 0.62 miles of flight to the food source. What about the direction in which to fly? The direction of the dancing bee's straight scuttle in relation to gravity translates to the direction the bee has to fly in relation to the sun. So, if the returning bee scuttles straight up, this means "fly in the direction of the sun." If the dancing bee scuttles down, then that means fly in the direction opposite to the sun.

Bumble bees may not dance like honey bees, but they still communicate with their sisters when they return from successful foraging trips. When a bumble bee comes home after finding nectar for the first time, she will race around the nest like a maniac, bumping into and climbing over her sister bees. At some point she will stop to spit up the nectar she collected into a nectar storage pot, but then she will continue to race around, fanning her wings from time to time. As she does this, she releases a pheromone (a chemical signal) from her abdomen, which is thought to stimulate other bees in the nest to go out to forage. After a few minutes of running around, she will leave the nest again to return to the food source. Each time she returns to the nest with nectar she will run around and fan her wings, but over time she will run less and less and act less and less excited.

As a result of this performance, a number of other bumble bee workers leave the nest to forage, too. Unlike honey bees, who "dance" in figure eights, the original bumble bee's excited runs don't have any obvious patterns to show other bees the distance and direction to go to get to the source of nectar she found. Each bumble bee forager must find flowers on her own; sometimes this results in other bumble bees finding the same flowers as the original running bumble bee, and sometimes not. The particular scent of the nectar from the returning bumble bee is thought to be all the information the new foragers have to go on. Still, for a bumble bee who has never left the nest to forage before, knowing what scent to search for in the world can save it a lot of time and energy, allowing it to avoid searching for good flowers strictly on a trial-and-error basis.

So bumble bees are unique from solitary and honey bees in terms of their life cycle, the amount of honey they store, and their communication within the nest. One thing that they have in common with these other species of bees, however, is their ability to sting![7] Bees are famous for their ability to sting. But bumble bees, and pretty much all other species of stinging bees, will only sting if given a reason; for example, if you swat at them or disturb their nest. Bumble bees will let you watch them if you don't get too close and don't breathe on them.[8]

The stingers of bumble bees are smooth, allowing them to sting repeatedly if they wish, and stinging does no harm to them. The stinger of a honey bee, on the other hand, has spikes, and gets stuck in the skin of mammals, including humans! After a honey bee stings, when she flies away, her sting, venom sac, and a large portion of her guts are yanked out and remain behind, and the honey bee dies. So, a honey bee can only sting you once, and once she does, she dies. (I say "she" because male honey bees—and male bumble bees, too—don't have a stinger, so they cannot sting.) Honey bee stingers don't seem to get stuck like that in other bees, so honey bees can sting other bees repeatedly.

---

7. There are in fact a large number of "stingless" species of bees, mostly found in tropical areas of the world.

8. In all my years working with bumble bees, I have never been stung.

Many hours of observation, from many different people, over many years, resulted in all that we know about bumble bees. And we continue to learn more about bumble bees today. Two people from the past, in particular, are best known for their early contributions to our storehouse of bumble bee knowledge.

DARWIN AND "BUZZING PLACES"

You may know Charles Darwin because of his groundbreaking book, *On the Origin of Species*, published in 1859, and his theory of evolution by natural selection. However, Darwin, with the help of his children, also spent a

FIGURE 2-2. Charles Darwin, around the year 1854.

considerable amount of time studying bumble bees—or "humble-bees," as they were referred to at that time.

It was Darwin's son Georgy who first spotted some bumble bees coming and going from a hole at the base of an ash tree near their home. Thinking that there must be a bumble bee nest there, Darwin and Georgy peered into the hole. Nothing. They removed all the grass and plants that were growing around it. Still no nest. They did notice, however, that more bumble bees would enter the hole, one by one, and then fly up and away between two large branches of the ash tree—each bumble bee flying the same path. When Darwin and Georgy followed the bumble bees, they saw that each bee would stop and hover for a few seconds at particular points along their route: first at a bare spot at the side of a ditch, and then at a spot several yards down over a particular ivy leaf. Darwin called these spots "buzzing places." He also noted that all of the bumble bees were male garden bumble bees.

Darwin and Georgy soon discovered the challenge of chasing flying bumble bees. The bumble bees flew along a ditch covered by a thick hedge, which was too overgrown for an adult to get through. Darwin had to recruit more of his children (he had seven in total) and had them all lie on their bellies at various points in the ditch to help track the bees. After discovering several more buzzing places, he tracked bumble bees by stationing each child close to one. He then had each one call out, "Here is a bee," as soon as a bee started buzzing around. The call of "Here is a bee" passed down the line of buzzing places until the bee reached the buzzing places where Darwin himself stood. Another one of Darwin's bee-tracking strategies consisted of having himself or one of his children sprinkle flour on a bee that had paused to buzz at a buzzing place. The white powder made it easier to see the bee as it flew, and it didn't seem to bother the bee at all.

This buzzing place study was great fun for the children, and even for Darwin. Darwin kept field notes and began to notice a few things. First, different bees, even bees born in different years, would visit the same buzzing places, often in the same sequence. There was also nothing special about the buzzing places; even when Darwin changed the appearance of the buzzing places by removing grass or plants or by sprinkling flour, the bees still paused to buzz at the same spots. Darwin also noticed that the bumble bees often flew near to the ground, along hedges or paths and at the base of trees. Besides garden bumble bees, Darwin and his children also observed male early bumble bees (*Bombus pratorum*)[9] and white-tailed bumble bees (*Bombus lucorum*) behaving in the same way.

Darwin and his children studied buzzing places for several years, from 1854 to 1861. It is a mystery why they abandoned their project, and Darwin never published his observations. The buzzing places remained a puzzle. What was so special about them? How did the male bumble bees identify them, even after Darwin changed their

---

9.   The early bumble bee got its name from being one of the first bumble bee species to emerge from hibernation in spring to start their nests.

appearance? Even male bumble bees of different generations paused at the same buzzing places. At one point in his field notes Darwin wrote, "Is it like dogs at cornerstones?" This refers to the fact that dogs pee to mark their territory, leaving behind a scent message for other dogs. Do male bumble bees mark buzzing places with a scent for other bees?

Many years later, scientists discovered that Darwin wasn't far off. Buzzing places are in fact marked with a pheromone that comes from a gland inside the male bumble bee's head, called the labial gland. The male bumble bees "paint" the pheromone onto objects, such as leaves or sticks or trees, using the bushy mustache around their mandibles. (When Darwin and his children moved things from the buzzing places, they must have moved things that were not marked by the bees, or the bees may have marked a lot of things in each area so that if one thing was moved, it didn't make any difference.) It turns out that these pheromones differ among different species of male bumble bees. Also, bumble bee species differ in terms of the height at which they create their flight paths and buzzing places. For example, male garden bumble bees tend to fly close to the ground, which would have made it easier for Darwin and his children to spot them.

What could be the point of buzzing places? Darwin

and scientists since his time believe that male bumble bees use them to attract a mate. The pheromones that male bumble bees paint on the buzzing places could attract queen bumble bees that need to mate before they hibernate for the winter. By patrolling the same route over and over, male bumble bees might eventually run into a queen. The different pheromones and different flight heights between species are thought to exist so that male bumble bees mate with their same species of queen.

The funny thing is that no one, not even Darwin and his children, has ever reported seeing a queen bumble bee hanging out at a buzzing place. There have also been no reports of male bumble bees running into a queen as they are flying along their route between buzzing places. In fact, witnessing a male bumble bee and a queen bumble bee mating in the wild is extremely rare. We're not sure why. Perhaps bumble bees are quite private when it comes to that behavior!

"Buzzing places" was not the only peculiar behavior Darwin observed in bumble bees. He saw that female bumble bees have a trick up their sleeve, too.

DARWIN AND NECTAR ROBBERS

In his rather less-well-known book, *On the Effects of Cross and Self Fertilization in the Vegetable Kingdom*, Darwin wrote about how he saw a number of bumble bees chew holes in the base of tube-shaped flowers and suck the flowers' nectar through these holes. This can be considered "cheating," as the bumble bee does not enter the flower in the usual way. It also usually results in the flower not being pollinated properly. Darwin saw that not only did bumble bees that returned to the same flowers continue to suck nectar through the holes, but other bumble bees and even honey bees used the existing holes as well.

Nowadays this strategy of biting holes in tube-shaped flowers is referred to as nectar robbing. The bees that first bite the holes are called primary nectar robbers, and the bees that reuse the holes are called secondary nectar robbers.[10] A primary nectar robber can also be a secondary nectar robber. Why do bees do this? Are they lazy and don't want to crawl into a flower to get its nectar? Darwin suggested that indeed nectar robbing could be saving the bee time, "for they lose much time in climbing into and out of large flowers, and in forcing their heads into closed ones." This is especially true for short-tongued bumble bees such as buff-tailed bumble bees, because their tongue is too short to reach the flower's nectar unless they crawl inside. And in fact, buff-tails are notorious for nectar-robbing,

---

10.   During a trip to Ireland, I saw buff-tailed bumble bees robbing flowers in people's gardens. I saw both primary and secondary robbers. I could hear the *click-click-click* of the primary robbers' mandibles as they chewed their way through the flowers' nectar tubes and saw the holes that they made in the flowers.

FIGURE 2-3. A buff-tailed bumble bee queen nectar-robbing a flower.

whereas the long-tongued garden bumble bee has rarely been seen robbing flowers. Honey bees have relatively short tongues, so it makes sense that they would be secondary nectar robbers, using the shortcut of a hole in the flower if one is available (although honey bees have sometimes been seen chewing their own holes in flowers).

Of course bumble bees don't always rob nectar from tube-shaped flowers; many bumble bees extract the flowers' nectar "legitimately" by climbing inside and probing the flower with their tongue. So, how does a bumble bee decide whether or not to rob a flower? This question hasn't been fully answered yet. However, one interesting finding is that sometimes, a "legitimate" forager forages from a flower that has a hole made by a primary nectar robber, and the bumble bee will switch to become a primary nectar robber themselves. On the other hand, if the "legitimate" foragers never encounter flowers with nectar-robber holes in them, they are much less likely to start robbing flowers. This suggests that bumble bees can learn food-gathering tricks from other bumble bees: In this case, they learned the "shortcut" of chewing a hole in a flower to get nectar.

MR. HUMBLE-BEE

Darwin wasn't the only one to be captivated by bumble bees back in the late 1800s and early 1900s. Frederick William Lambert Sladen, who, like Darwin, lived in the United Kingdom, published the first comprehensive book about bumble bees in 1912, entitled, *The Humble-Bee: Its Life History and How to Domesticate It.* In this book, Sladen

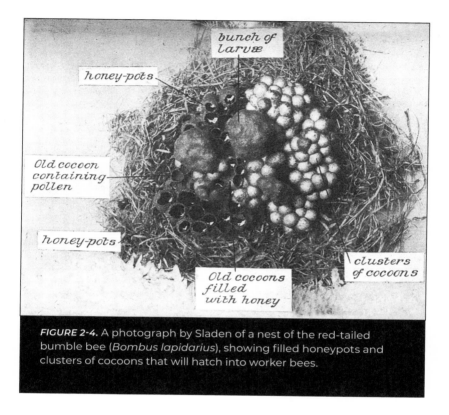

FIGURE 2-4. A photograph by Sladen of a nest of the red-tailed bumble bee (*Bombus lapidarius*), showing filled honeypots and clusters of cocoons that will hatch into worker bees.

provides oodles of details about the life cycle of a bumble bee colony and how to distinguish the various species of bumble bees found in Britain, and he recounts his many entertaining attempts to observe and raise bumble bees on his own. The first thing he had to do, though, was find bumble bee nests.

Sladen spent many hours looking for and digging up underground bumble bee nests, and then transferring the nests to a place where he could more closely observe them. He would put the nest on the ground ("any convenient part of the garden will do," he wrote), surround the colony with a good supply of moss or blades of grass, and then cover the colony with a box

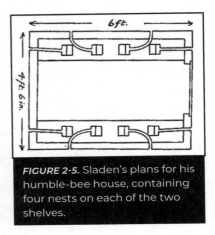

FIGURE 2-5. Sladen's plans for his humble-bee house, containing four nests on each of the two shelves.

or upside-down flower pot to protect it from sun and rain. By lifting up the box or flower pot, he could observe the goings-on in the nest.

Sladen was so invested in watching bumble bees that he constructed what he called a "humble-bee house": a six-foot by four-foot wooden shack in his backyard. Inside the humble-bee house were two shelves, one on each side, extending along the length of the humble-bee house. On each shelf there were four wooden boxes with a glass top; the glass top allowed him to see inside. In each box Sladen placed a bumble bee nest that he had dug up from his property. There was a tube from each bee-box leading to the outside, so that the bumble bees could come and go freely to collect food. A window in Sladen's humble-bee house gave him enough light to watch the bumble bees during the day. When he was not watching the bees, he covered the window with a thick black blind. This was to mimic the darkness of natural underground bumble bee nests. In the evenings Sladen observed the bumble bees by candlelight.

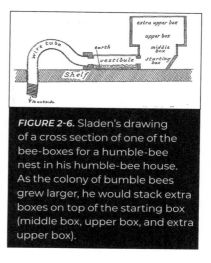

FIGURE 2-6. Sladen's drawing of a cross section of one of the bee-boxes for a humble-bee nest in his humble-bee house. As the colony of bumble bees grew larger, he would stack extra boxes on top of the starting box (middle box, upper box, and extra upper box).

At one point, Sladen went so far as to keep one of the wooden boxes of bumble bees in his study. He describes how he kept the box with the nest on a table in the room. If the weather outside was nice, he left a window in his study open during the day, and left the bumble bee box open, so that worker bumble bees could come and go as they pleased. The bumble bees would fly straight to the window when leaving and fly straight back to the box upon their return. When the worker bees returned, large balls of pollen could often be seen on their back legs. Sladen closed the study window in the evening once all of the worker bees were back at the nest. If it was very windy outside or raining, Sladen would keep the nest and study window closed for the day and give the bumble bees some honey to tide them over until the weather improved and the bees could go outside to forage for nectar for themselves.

The bumble bees had lived peacefully in Sladen's study for several days, when suddenly the workers were thrown into a frenzy. Sladen wrote that "They rushed madly over the comb, attacking and pushing one another with great vehemence, and half their comrades were on the floor idle and drowsy." Sladen tried to restore order to the nest by removing five of the most violent worker bees, but the colony remained in a state of mayhem. Then he noticed that the queen did not look well. She seemed oblivious to the chaos around her and to have "fallen into a kind of stupor." Sladen tried to wake her, but she only trembled and would not sip any of the honey that he gave her. Then the worker bumble bees pounced on her. As Sladen wrote, "A worker seized one of her hind legs in her jaws and began pulling it, another tugged at one of her antennae, and a third caught hold of her tongue and tried to drag her along by it. She did not seem to mind this rough treatment, but slowly cleaned her antennae with her foreleg when the worker let go. Probably she was only half conscious. Evidently the object of the workers in seizing her was not to attack her but to remove her; they seemed to have decided that she was useless and going to die."

Sure enough, the queen died the next day. Sladen notes that in all cases in which he saw a colony of bumble bees lose its queen, the workers would descend into chaos, attacking one another, often to the death. The reason? "They fight to become mothers," Sladen explained. Someone needs to replace the queen. Without a queen, worker bumble bees can start laying eggs. Left to its own devices, Sladen discovered that a queenless colony soon calms down and is ruled by one or more worker bumble bees, yet there is still occasional fighting. In one case Sladen found fourteen dead worker bees from a nest of about sixty bees!

What happened to the bumble bee colony in Sladen's study after it lost its queen? There were always a large number of bumble bee nests on Sladen's property that he kept his eye on. He found a nest of the same bumble bee species (the red-tailed bumble bee) that was not very big and had a healthy queen. He dug it up and united it with the colony in his study. The new bumble bees made themselves at home right away, and the original bumble bees welcomed them with open wings. Sladen described the introduction as follows:

> [The queen] was pleased to find herself in so large and prosperous a colony, and after running over the brood and hugging it she went to a honeypot and took a long draught. All the workers that approached her seemed interested in her, waving their antennae in her direction or touching her, but none attempted

to attack her, and they soon seemed to regard her presence as a matter of course; they also ceased to butt one another and peace was restored.

There were some bumps in this new relationship, however. Sladen describes that there were some worker bumble bees that would rip open the wax cells where the new queen had laid some eggs, and if the queen did not successfully shoo the workers away, they would end up eating the eggs. The queen often had to contend with mischievous, egg-eating workers; some she was able to fend off, others not so much. Perhaps these worker bees were not as accepting of their new queen, unlike the rest of the colony, and they attempted to sabotage the new queen's egg-laying efforts. However, the queen managed to reign over the colony for the full season until late summer, when bumble bee colonies usually start dying off.

Sladen was very successful in learning how to observe and care for bumble bee colonies outdoors, in his humble-bee house, and inside in his study—and he provided many details in his book that would allow others to follow in his footsteps.

Still, Sladen longed for "complete domestication" of bumble bees. By this he meant that they would become pets and live with humans and depend upon us, like cats and dogs. The piece of the puzzle that eluded him was

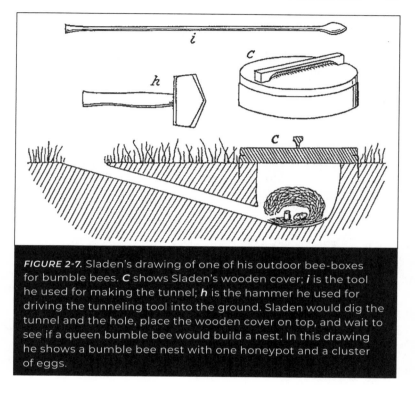

FIGURE 2-7. Sladen's drawing of one of his outdoor bee-boxes for bumble bees. **C** shows Sladen's wooden cover; *i* is the tool he used for making the tunnel; *h* is the hammer he used for driving the tunneling tool into the ground. Sladen would dig the tunnel and the hole, place the wooden cover on top, and wait to see if a queen bumble bee would build a nest. In this drawing he shows a bumble bee nest with one honeypot and a cluster of eggs.

how to mimic or avoid the hibernation that queen bumble bees undergo over the winter so that he could study them all year. In late summer and early fall, the eggs and larvae in bumble bee colonies develop into males and new queens. The males and queens leave the nest, mate, the males die, and the queens burrow into the earth where they will sleep for the winter. In spring, the queens emerge, find a nest, and start their own colonies. Sladen had no problem getting queen and male bumble bees to mate. However, afterward, when he provided the mated queens some loose dirt in which to bury themselves, they either refused, or, if they did manage to find a spot and fall asleep, they woke up when Sladen checked on them. Then they either died or flew away. Sladen wrote that "Evidently the least disturbance causes the queens to evacuate their hiding-places."

After Sladen published his book, he continued to devote his working life to bees. In 1912, the same year his book came out, Sladen moved to Canada to start a job studying bees for the Canadian government. He soon became their top bee scientist. At the time, his work focused on honey bees, since understanding them was important to using them to pollinate farmers' crops. Sadly, Sladen passed away on September 10, 1921, at the age of forty-five. At the time, he was conducting honey bee experiments on Duck Island in Ontario, Canada, and he had apparently been having heart trouble for several years beforehand. It is believed he took a break from his studies, went into the water to bathe, suffered a heart attack, and died.

Darwin's and Sladen's careful observations paved the way for the future relationship between humans and bumble bees. Many decades later, scientists continue Darwin's work on bumble bee mating and food-finding behaviors. Eventually, Sladen's mystery of how to completely raise bumble bees under human control was solved. As we will see, this accomplishment in particular resulted in the very existence of bumble bees being altered forever.

CHAPTER THREE

Super Bees

Decades after Sladen's untimely death, researchers and bumble bee enthusiasts were still using his techniques from the early 1900s to raise their own bumble bee colonies. They would capture queen bumble bees that were buzzing around outdoors in the spring, for these queens would have just emerged from hibernation and would be ready to start their own colony. Each captured queen was released into a cage or greenhouse to see whether she would start laying eggs. Another technique involved releasing males and queens into a cage to mate, and then providing trays filled with loose dirt or peat where the queens could bury themselves. This was somewhat successful. But no matter how these colonies were created, people were still tied to the seasonal life cycle of the bumble bee: They needed to wait months for queens to emerge from hibernation, ready to start their nests. How could they avoid this and breed bumble bee colonies year-round?

If they could figure out how to make queen bumble bees lay eggs and start colonies at any time of year, this would allow them to study and learn about bumble bees any time they wanted. But also, as we will see, this would be an incredible opportunity for farmers around the world who could use bumble bees to pollinate their crops.

IT ALL BEGAN WITH . . . CUCUMBERS

Jan Koppert loved cucumbers. Each day he would tend to his crop, thinking about how he could help his plants grow cucumbers that were bigger, plumper, and more numerous. Unfortunately, there were many diseases and pests that attacked his crop. It was 1967, and chemicals were available that Koppert could spray onto his cucumber plants to protect them. But the tiny bugs that ate his cucumbers soon became resistant to these treatments. Spraying the chemicals in a warm, enclosed greenhouse was extremely unhealthy for Koppert, too. Soon he became allergic to the pest-control products and they made him very sick. He faced a tough decision: find another way to protect his cucumbers, or quit the cucumber business altogether.

Koppert didn't want to give up on his passion. He started researching natural enemies of one particular pest that was infesting his cucumbers: spider mites. He eventually discovered tiny creatures related to spiders and ticks that attack and feed on spider mites. They were called predatory mites. He found a chemical company that had some of them on hand. So, he took a train from his home in the Netherlands to Dielsdorf, Switzerland, to pick up some of these predatory mites.

The Swiss company's research department gave Koppert several dozen leaves that had the predatory mites on them. He very carefully brought the leaves and mites home and bred the mites in a small greenhouse behind his home. They multiplied. When he released this "army" onto his cucumber crop, they worked like a charm! His cucumbers were safe. Koppert continued to breed and use the predatory mites. He even started to sell them to other local growers. His company, Koppert Biological Systems, was born.[1]

Sadly, Koppert became very sick and passed away in 1972, not long after he made his breakthrough with the mites. His sons took over the company, and they discovered and sold a number of natural crop treatments. Koppert Biological Systems continues to be a successful worldwide business today.

So where do bumble bees come in? Well, around 1987,

---

1. Koppert Biological Systems still sells the same type of predatory mites that Koppert began breeding in the 1960s. The product is called Spidex. It comes in different-sized bottles filled with wood chips and the mites.

Koppert's sons heard of a veterinarian in Belgium who was breeding bumble bees. This sparked their interest, because they immediately saw huge advantages of branching out into the bumble bee business. First, they expected farmers, especially farmers of greenhouse tomatoes, to pounce on the opportunity to use bumble bees to pollinate their crops. Up to that point in time, the process of pollinating greenhouse tomato blossoms had been quite complicated. Three times a week, people would go from plant to plant, vibrating the pollen loose from each flower using a handheld, mechanical device that looked like a giant electric toothbrush. This was an expensive job that cost over $11,000 per hectare[2] per year! An alternative was to treat the tomato plants with hormones. Bumble bees seemed like a much more natural, simpler, and less costly strategy.

The Kopperts also realized that if farmers placed colonies of bumble bees near their crops, they would have to be careful about what treatments they applied to the plants. Specifically, they could no longer spray their crops with chemicals, or else they would risk killing the bumble bees. The farmers would instead have to rely on safer, more natural means of pest control—which is what Koppert Biological Systems provided. It certainly seemed like a win-win situation.

---

2.   One hectare contains about 2.47 acres. The grassy area inside of a standard running track is a little over one hectare in size.

The Koppert brothers took the trek from the Netherlands to Belgium to meet this veterinarian-turned-bumble-bee-breeder. The veterinarian's name was Dr. Roland de Jonghe, and he had been fascinated by bumble bees since he was a little boy. As a hobby, he was now breeding bumble bees in his backyard, garage, and even in his living room. One day, Dr. de Jonghe saw a bumble bee that happened to get inside of his friend's greenhouse, and the bumble bee was pollinating a tomato plant. Just like the Koppert brothers, inspiration struck him: What if bumble bees could be bred and sold to greenhouse tomato farmers? Gone would be the difficult, expensive task of pollinating tomatoes by hand.

The brothers and Dr. de Jonghe learned that they had the same realizations and the same ideas about selling bumble bees to greenhouse tomato farmers. They chatted, but rather than work together, they went their separate ways. Dr. de Jonghe started his own company, Biobest. Both Dr. de Jonghe and the Koppert brothers eventually solved the mystery of how to avoid the need for bumble bee queens to hibernate, thereby allowing them to breed bumble bee queens year-round. How they do this is still a tightly kept secret.

Both Biobest and Koppert Biological Systems set up factory-like conditions to start mass-producing bumble bee colonies by the hundreds, and then by the thousands. Each bumble bee colony was placed in a plastic box with a cardboard outer box, given a supply of pollen and sugar water (as a substitute for flower nectar), and then sealed up and mailed to its destination. Sales went through the roof. They shipped bumble bee colonies across countries. It was a new dawn for agriculture, and for bumble bees as well.

WHAT IS POLLINATION, ANYWAY?

Fruits and vegetables such as blueberries, tomatoes, and sweet peppers start out as flowers. The flowers make tiny grains called pollen. The pollen looks like dust and can be a variety of different colors, depending on the type of flower it comes from: yellow, orange, white, and even purple. Some plants can make more than one pollen color and sometimes very different species of plants can produce the same pollen color. Why does pollen come in so many different varieties? One reason may be that the color, or pigment, of the pollen protects it from being damaged by heat from sunlight. For example, scientists found that the American bellflower makes different pollen colors depending on where it grows: Its pollen is tan-colored in more eastern, cooler areas and is dark purple in more western, warmer areas. When the scientists exposed the variety of pollen to heat, the purple pollen was able to resist higher temperatures, whereas the tan-colored pollen became damaged: It could no longer allow the plant to reproduce.

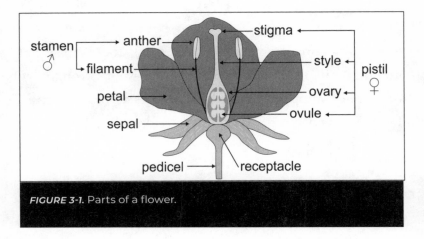

FIGURE 3-1. Parts of a flower.

The darker, purple color is thought to somehow protect the pollen from the hotter climate. Another reason for different pollen colors is to attract pollinators—like bumble bees!

In order for the flower to grow into a fruit or vegetable, the pollen must be moved from one part of the flower to another: The pollen is made in the anthers, and it must be moved to the stigma (see Figure 3-1).

One way that pollen can be moved is to have animals, like bumble bees, visit the flower. When an animal visits the flower for nectar, their body rubs up against the anther, and they become dusted in pollen. Then, as the animal moves, they might bump up against the stigma, which is often sticky, and pollen grains are transferred from the animal's body to the stigma. So, in a way, bumble bees and other animals pollinate flowers by accident.

Plants tend to make even better fruits or vegetables if the pollen is transferred from the anthers of one flower to the stigma of another. But the flowers must be the same type. For example, blueberry flowers can only be pollinated by other blueberry flowers. So as a bumble bee visits many flowers of the same type, she is helping to make good food for us.

But how do creatures find the flowers? Flowers that need to be pollinated look attractive to pollinators. For example, flowers that are pollinated by bees often have petals that have a flat landing surface, as well as an attractive smell and bright colors. They also provide nectar for the bees, which is the reason the bees visit flowers in the first place: to get food.

When a bumble bee becomes covered in pollen grains, she uses her legs to scrape the pollen grains from her fur to her corbiculae (pollen baskets) on her back legs. She packs the pollen into balls, kind of like making a ball out of play-dough. Her legs might not be able to reach all of the pollen grains, though, so some might still be on her fur. When she visits the next flower, these stray pollen grains may rub off onto the flower, and voilà! Pollination.

When the bumble bee returns to the nest, she scrapes the balls of pollen off her back legs, and that pollen will be used to feed the larvae.

Although a number of different animals can pollinate

flowers (as we learned in Chapter One), there are several reasons why bumble bees are some of the best pollinators around.

BUMBLE BEES: SUPERSTAR POLLINATORS

Many different animals pollinate flowers: butterflies, hummingbirds, bats, beetles, flies, and other types of bees, such as honey bees. Some plants are even pollinated by the wind! The wind blows pollen grains from one plant to another. As we saw earlier in this chapter, even humans can pollinate flowers by hand.

Honey bees are undoubtedly the most widely used pollinators for food crops around the world. Each honey bee colony produces thousands of worker bees that can pollinate enormous areas. There is an abundance of information and expertise for farmers on how to successfully manage honey bee colonies. And, of course, honey bees provide honey, which farmers can also sell.

However, honey bees are not the best pollinators. For one thing, they are "fair-weather foragers," meaning they will usually not leave the hive to pollinate crops if it is cold or rainy outside. Honey bees also have short tongues, making them less likely to visit crops that have flowers with deep nectar tubes. It is also very risky to depend on only one species of pollinator to pollinate a crop, in case disease or some other event spreads throughout the colonies. As we will see in

Chapter Five, something known as colony collapse disorder led to a serious decline in the number of commercial honey bees, leaving some without pollinators for their plants.[3]

Meanwhile, bumble bees can be considered superstar pollinators for several reasons. They have much more fur that the pollen can stick to, and so the pollen can be moved to the stigmas of other flowers. And because bumble bees are covered in thick fur, they can stay out in cooler weather. Often bumble bees will be out foraging on colder days when other insects are not.

Bumble bees can also do a cool trick that honey bees can't, called buzz pollination. (Scientists also call it sonication.) In some flowers, like those of tomato or blueberry plants, the pollen is more hidden inside the anthers: There might only be a slit where the pollen can come out. When a bumble bee lands on these flowers, she grabs the bottom of the anthers with her mandibles and curls her whole body around the anthers. Then she vibrates her flight muscles really fast. As the bee shakes her muscles, the anthers shake, too, causing the pollen grains to fall out and onto the bumble bee's belly. This is kind of like when we shake a tree to make the fruit fall down. It's called buzz pollination because when the bumble bee vibrates her flight muscles it makes a

---

3.   *Decline* refers to the shrinking of the number of bees (or other animals) found on the planet.

loud buzz sound. This buzz sounds a bit different from the buzzing the bumble bee makes when she flies: It's shorter (only a second or two) and is a bit higher pitched. If you ever get a chance to hang around tomato or blueberry plants when there are bumble bees flying about, listen for the "buzz" of buzz pollination![4]

Buzz pollination is a rather big deal. It happens to approximately twenty thousand plant species. Usually little brown marks are left on the anther after it has been buzz pollinated. Commercial tomato growers call these marks bee kisses, and they are a sign that bees have visited the flowers.

WHAT TYPES OF CROPS ARE POLLINATED BY BUMBLE BEES?

When tomato plants are buzz pollinated by bumble bees, they produce better fruit. So naturally, the number one crop that is pollinated by bumble bees is the greenhouse tomato. Around the world, 95 percent of all bumble bee sales are for pollinating greenhouse tomatoes. The value of this bumble-bee-pollinated crop is estimated to be about $14 billion per year.

---

4.   Scientists took high-speed videos of an Australian bee, the blue-banded bee (*Amegilla murrayensis*), while the bees were foraging on cherry tomato plants. They saw that, like bumble bees, this bee grasped the anthers of the tomato plants with its legs, but it didn't grasp it with its mandibles. Instead, when the blue-banded bee shook its flight muscles, its head banged up against the anthers of the blossom over and over. This tapping of its head released the pollen. Head-banging bees!

Other things you might see in your local grocery store that are pollinated by commercial bumble bees include peppers (both sweet and hot), eggplant, melon, watermelon, cucumber, zucchini, strawberry, raspberry, blackberry, currant (red and black), cranberry, blueberry, apple, pear, cherry, kiwi, peach, apricot, and plum. Honey bees can also be used to pollinate these crops, but they can often be less efficient than bumble bees.

WHY IS POLLINATION SUCH A BIG DEAL?

Take a moment to think about all the fruits and vegetables that you and other people eat. Then add on seeds, nuts, and oils. All of these foods come from crops that need to be pollinated. In fact, one in three bites of food would not exist if it weren't for bees and other pollinators. Next time you eat a meal, look at your own plate. Or take a look inside your refrigerator. How much of the food do you think relies on pollination?

Our dependence on pollinators has been increasing substantially over time. Over the past fifty years, we have planted so many more crops that we have tripled the amount of crops that need pollination. Plus, the human population is expected to continue to increase, so much so that in order to feed everyone, the land needed for more food crops is expected to double between 2005 and 2050.

Some scientists suggest that growing food in greenhouses

can be a potential solution for this demand, because greenhouses allow for larger quantities of high-quality food to be grown in less space using minimal amounts of fertilizer, labor, water, and energy. If we do end up building more greenhouses to grow more crops to try to prevent food shortages, this means we will need more commercial bumble bee colonies to pollinate all those extra crops.

And our food crops are not the only ones that are reliant on pollination: Almost 90 percent of all wild flowering plants need animal pollination in order to survive.

SECRETS SURROUNDING COMMERCIAL BUMBLE BEES

So with pollinators in such high demand, how are Biobest and Koppert Biological Systems doing, in terms of their sales of commercial bumble bee colonies?[5] That is a very good question. How they get queen bumble bees to skip the hibernation process is not the only secret they keep. There are no recent reports available anywhere that give any indication of how many bumble bee colonies they sell. When asked how many they sell each year, each company said it was "confidential information," or "close to one million colonies a year." No other details. There was a report published

---

5.   There are a number of other commercial bumble bee companies around the world, but Biobest and Koppert Biological Systems are the biggest.

back in 2006, however, that suggests that the number of commercial colonies shipped around the world each year is . . . a lot.

Figure 3-2 is taken from that report. It is a graph showing how many bumble bees were sold worldwide, from all companies combined, between the years 1988 and 2004. In 1988 there were no bumble bee colonies sold because that was the year the companies were just getting started. But once bumble bee production began, there was a steady increase in colony sales each year until sales reached *one million* colonies in 2004! The common eastern bumble bee (*Bombus impatiens*) was the main species sold for pollination within North America, whereas the buff-tailed bumble bee was the main species sold elsewhere.

Have bumble bee sales continued to increase since 2004, as the graph seems to suggest? We can't conclude anything until we have data from the commercial companies, and they are keeping that information close to their chests. However, there is no indication that things have slowed down since that report was released in 2006. According to Biobest's website, they now provide bumble bee colonies to nearly seventy countries around the world. Koppert Biological Systems doesn't look that far behind. It's pretty safe to say that the commercial bumble bee business is booming.

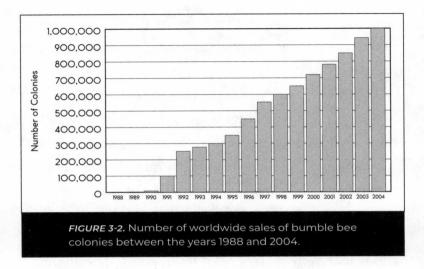

FIGURE 3-2. Number of worldwide sales of bumble bee colonies between the years 1988 and 2004.

Besides keeping busy selling thousands of bumble bee colonies, these companies test new ideas for pollination. Two discoveries were made that make their bumble bees extra effective for farmers. First, they found that male bumble bees can be master pollinators themselves, and as a result, Biobest sells a product called the Masculino-System. It consists of a box of about fifty male buff-tailed bumble bees, which farmers can release onto their crops. And second, bumble bees can not only pollinate plants but can be used to deliver treatments to them.

MALE BUMBLE BEES AS POLLINATORS?

Until recently it was thought that male bumble bees were only good for mating with queen bumble bees. Remember that after male bumble bees hatch, they stay in the nest and eat until they are strong enough to leave. After they leave, they find a queen bumble bee to mate with, and then they die. It has always been assumed that female worker bumble bees are the better pollinators because they visit a lot of flowers in order to bring back lots of nectar and pollen to the nest. Male bumble bees, on the other hand, only visit enough flowers to keep themselves fed with nectar until they find a mate. However, male bumble bees actually have some advantages over female bumble bees as pollinators.

Male bumble bees have more fur than female bumble bees, so there is more fur for the pollen grains to stick to. Male bumble bees also don't have corbiculae on their back legs like female bumble bees, and they don't collect pollen. They only need nectar for energy. So, when their fur becomes covered in pollen grains, they don't scrape it all back into pellets on their back legs like females do. This means that the pollen grains are loosely attached all over their body, making it easier for them to be transferred to another flower. In other words, it's likely that more loose pollen travels on a male bumble bee's body compared to a female's body when visiting flowers and more can rub off onto other flowers.

In the late summer and early fall, the female worker bumble bees die off, but there are many more males remaining. These males visit plants that are "late bloomers" that flower at that time of year, which female bumble bees miss. When flying between these flowers, male bumble bees probably fly longer distances since they don't need to collect as much nectar as female bumble bees do. This means that pollen can be transferred between a bigger variety of plants, which usually results in better fruit compared to pollen being transferred to flowers within the same plant.

A group of scientists ran a few experiments to test these points. They counted the number of male bumble bees, female bumble bees, and queen bumble bees on flowering plants along a hiking trail in late summer. Then they watched male and female bumble bees collect nectar from patches of artificial flowers in their laboratory. Afterward, they compared the amount of pollen that male and female bumble bees transferred between real flowers that they grew in their lab.

What the scientists found was that there were in fact more male bumble bees on the flowering plants along the hiking trails at that time of year compared to the number of female worker bumble bees and queens. They also saw that male bumble bees tended to fly between patches of artificial flowers to collect nectar more often than visiting flowers within a patch. In other words, the male bees tended to fly farther distances compared to the females to collect nectar. Finally, the scientists determined that male bees did transfer more pollen between the flowers. Not only that, but they spent more time at each flower (what scientists call a greater flower handling time). Spending more time at a particular flower means that there is more chance for pollen grains to be transferred to that flower.

So, although male bumble bees visit fewer flowers than female bumble bees, it seems as though they can transfer more pollen between flower visits compared to female bumble bees, and they can transfer pollen between flowers that are farther apart. This nicely complements the pollination that female bumble bees do. And all this time we thought that male bumble bees were only good for mating!

SPECIAL DELIVERY BY BUMBLE BEES

Pollen might not be the only thing that ends up clinging to a bee's fur when it visits a flower. On their travels, bees have been known to pick up tiny critters that we can't see with the naked eye, which can spread disease and infection to plants and other bees. Some clever scientists came up with an idea: If bees can spread stuff that's bad for plants and bees, why can't they also spread stuff that can *benefit* them?

People had been looking for more natural ways to protect their crops from various pests and things that can cause disease. That way they wouldn't have to rely on chemical sprays. This was particularly the case when farmers started using commercial bumble bees to pollinate greenhouse plants: Pesticide sprays that are usually applied to crops could greatly harm or kill their bees. Also, by using more natural ways to control crop pests and diseases, they would no longer need to worry about chemical residues sticking around on harvested food.

The idea was pretty simple: Before a bee leaves her nest to forage, we could get her to walk through some powder that contained a microscopic fungus[6] or other type of creature mixed into it that could fight off plant pests. The bee would become dusted in the powder, and when she lands on a flower to collect its pollen and/or nectar, the dust would rub off onto the flower, protecting it from harm.

There were some challenges to overcome to make this successful, though. For one thing, what kind of powder should be used? It would have to be something that sticks pretty well to bee fur, because when a bee buzzes her wings and lifts off to fly, much of the powder could be shaken off. Also, bees are known to groom themselves: They actually lift up a leg or two and slide them over their fur, smoothing their fur down and at the same time scraping off anything

---

6.   *Microscopic* means that it is too small to see without a microscope. A *fungus* (plural *fungi*) belongs to a kingdom of living organisms that are separate from animals and plants. They spread spores, which are similar to seeds, to allow them to reproduce, but are usually too small to see. Fungi include mushrooms, yeasts, and molds, and many fungi can only be seen with a microscope. Some types of fungi are harmful to bumble bees.

that might be stuck to it.[7] If a bee became dusted in powder, she might find this irritating and groom all or most of the powder off her body. There would then be none, or very little, left over to transfer to the flowers she visited.

Scientists tried out a number of different types of powders to see which type would stick to bee fur without irritating the bees too much: wheat flour, durum semolina, corn flour, potato starch, potato flakes, oat flour, and barley flour. Corn flour seemed to work best. More stayed on the bees' bodies and the bees groomed less.

After the best type of powder was identified, the researchers needed to design a dispenser that would cover the bees in as much powder as possible. The best type of dispenser seems to be a ramp or tray with a layer of powder that the bees have to walk through before exiting their nest. The tray can even have a number of pegs sticking up from the bottom so that the bee has to walk in a zigzag, obstacle-course path through the tray, resulting in the bee walking longer through the powder (and thus becoming more covered in powder), as opposed to walking through the tray in a straight line. And when the bees return to the nest after

---

7.   When I was a student studying bumble bees, I had to glue small, plastic, numbered discs to the thorax of bumble bees to tell them apart. Once I finished gluing a label onto a bee, she would often try to groom or scrape it off with her legs. If I didn't let the glue dry enough, she would end up swiping the label off and I would have to start all over again.

foraging, they enter through a different hole. This is so that the bee doesn't walk through the powder again when she comes back, tracking the powder into the nest and wasting powder that could have gone to the flowers outside. (And living in a home that becomes increasingly dusty with powder would be quite annoying!)

One of the first tests of this system was back in 1992, using honey bees to deliver a special fungus to combat gray mold in strawberries. Gray mold looks exactly as it sounds: It starts off on the strawberry blossom, too small to see, but as the fruit grows and ripens, it becomes infected with a fuzzy gray mold, and the strawberry cannot be eaten. In the study, honey bees walked through a powder with the beneficial fungus spores mixed into it, and then pollinated the strawberry plants as usual. The scientists found that the honey bees were just as good, and perhaps even better, at delivering the treatment to the strawberry plants compared to using a spray. And the resulting fruit was relatively free of mold.

However, honey bees tend to forage less when the weather is not favorable, and the researchers noticed this in their study. Enter bumble bees!

A number of studies since the one that used honey bees have found that bumble bees are quite effective at delivering different types of naturally occurring fungi to control diseases and pests that affect strawberries, lowbush blueberries, and greenhouse sweet peppers and tomatoes. In some cases, the results were the same or even better than if the farmers had used chemical sprays. The fancy name given to the use of bumble bees (and other bees for that matter) to deliver plant treatments is pollinator biocontrol vector technology. The bees are known as vectors, since this word in biology refers to a living thing that transmits or carries something such as a fungus, bacterium, or virus.

Will this technology eventually replace the need for chemical pesticides? It certainly sounds like a good idea, and especially an environmentally friendly one. But this technology has a number of issues that need to be addressed first. For one thing, bumble bees are not the only pollinators that visit flowering crops. Will the plant treatments that bumble bees spread onto flowers hurt other beneficial insects? And what about the resulting fruit or vegetable that grows from the bumble-bee-treated flower? Will it be safe for us (and potentially other animals) to eat? Bumble bees might visit other flower species not meant for the treatment as well. Will the treatment harm other plants that become exposed to it? And finally, in all of the studies so far, bumble bees did not seem to be affected by the different types of fungus that they transported. But are there effects that don't necessarily kill the bees but still harm them in some way (what we call sublethal effects)? Are there any long-term health consequences to bees and their colonies if they are used to transport plant treatments? We have yet to find out for sure.

Whether or not bumble bees will eventually be used to rid farmers' crops of diseases and pests, the fact remains that we have realized the pollinating power of bumble bees. And we have taken advantage of that power: Bumble bee "factories" now exist worldwide, where we produce and ship bumble bee colonies around the globe by the thousands each year. The impact this has had on the food industry, and the ability to deliver better food to our tables, has been enormous. But that's not the only impact the bumble bee industry has had. As we will see, the price we are paying for mass-producing a species for our benefit is a steep one.

CHAPTER FOUR

Escape!

SNEAKY BEES

It was a typical day for a young research scientist in Southwestern British Columbia, Canada. She watched as worker bumble bees flew into their nest boxes, returning from pollen-gathering trips in the tomato plants that filled the greenhouse. Peering through the transparent plastic cover of the nest box, the scientist could see each returning bee scurry around in the nest with bright yellow balls of pollen attached to her back legs. The bees scraped off the pollen so that it could be fed to the larvae, and then flew out from the nest box to forage once again.

Bee after bee returned with pollen for the colony. But then the scientist noticed something strange: The color of the pollen wasn't always the same. Sometimes it was the usual distinctive yellow, but sometimes it was a different shade of yellow or a different color altogether. The scientist knew that different pollen colors meant the bees were gathering pollen from different types of flowers. But how could that be possible if the bees were in a greenhouse that only had tomato plants?

The scientist and her research team decided to investigate. At the original greenhouse and two others, they captured worker bumble bees at the entrance of their nest boxes when they returned from a foraging trip. After a bumble bee was caught, she was cooled on ice to make her drowsy while the researchers gently scraped the pollen off her back legs. The bee was then returned safely to her nest. Although the color of the pollen loads gave a clue as to which types of plant(s) the bumble bee collected it from, just to be certain, the researchers identified each of the collected pollen samples using a microscope.

The team collected pollen for eight months, between February and September. You might expect that because the bumble bee colonies were kept in greenhouses filled with tomato plants, all of the pollen collected by the bees would be tomato pollen. However, what the researchers found was quite surprising. At one of the greenhouses, bumble bees had brought back 95 percent tomato pollen; so 5 percent of their pollen was from plants outside of the greenhouse. That meant some of the bumble bees had been escaping from the greenhouse to collect pollen, but not many. But at another greenhouse, as much as 73 percent of the pollen samples were from non-tomato flowers! The foreign pollen was mainly from blackberry, raspberry, thimbleberry, salmonberry, and dandelion, although some of the pollen also came from thistle, foxglove, fireweed, buttercup, and pink spirea. All of these plant species bloomed in the area surrounding the greenhouses. Notably, throughout the course of the experiment, there was never a lack of tomato flowers in the greenhouses. The conclusion? Despite the availability of tomato flowers in the greenhouses, a large number of worker bumble bees were sneaking out through vents, cracks, or open windows and getting food elsewhere!

Besides the fact that farmers were not getting their full money's worth after purchasing bumble bees to pollinate their tomato crops, there is another consequence to escaped bees. Worker bumble bees always return to their nest; but later in the season when new queens and males emerge in the colony, these bees leave the nest for good to find a mate. If males and queens escape from greenhouses, they can establish colonies of bumble bees in the wild. This is exactly what happened in Japan, Chile, Argentina, western Canada, and the western United States. And as we will see, when this happened it was not just bumble bees that were introduced into these new territories.

ESCAPEE #1: THE BUFF-TAILED BUMBLE BEE

JAPAN

Beginning in 1991, Japanese companies began to import commercial colonies of buff-tailed bumble bees from Europe to pollinate greenhouse crops, mainly tomatoes. Buff-tails are not native to Japan; Japan does, however, have a number of species of wild bumble bees.

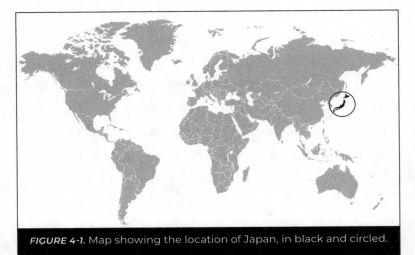

FIGURE 4-1. Map showing the location of Japan, in black and circled.

By 2004, Japan was importing around seventy thousand of these colonies every year. There were certainly going to be escapees, especially when researchers saw that during the time of year when males and new queens were ready to leave the nest, windows of greenhouses were left open and vents leading to the outside were not screened over. Sure enough, in 1996, a buff-tailed bumble bee nest was found in the wild in northern Japan. Soon after, there were reports of sightings of buff-tailed queens that had emerged from hibernation not far from agricultural areas where commercial colonies had been mass introduced. Within six years, buff-tailed queens were found about six miles away from the initial source. This foreign species was flourishing in their new land and had started to spread.

Scientists warned that these massive imports of a foreign bumble bee species could have major effects on the pollinators that are naturally found in Japan, as well as how the natural Japanese plants and animals interact with each other (what is called an ecosystem). For example, if introduced bumble bees escape into the natural environment, they can transmit diseases or infections to existing bumble bee species. Introduced buff-tailed queens and males might mate with other native species, creating hybrid species, which would change the genetic makeup of the natural bumble bee population. An invasion of buff-tailed bumble bees into the natural ecosystem could create competition with existing bumble bee species for nest sites and food, eventually pushing out the native bee species. Also, if buff-tails interfere with the abundance of natural Japanese bumble bee species, this could in turn interfere with the pollination of native plant species. This would be especially harmful if buff-tailed bumble bees mostly pollinate plant species that are not native to the country.

Unfortunately, these warnings went unheeded. In fact, the scientists' predictions were coming true. Researchers captured a great number of two types of wild bumble bee queens: what is known in Japan as the large bumble bee (*Bombus hypocrita hypocrita*), and the Ezo large bumble bee (*Bombus hypocrita sapporoensis*).[1] Many of the queens had mated with buff-tailed males. The result? The large bumble bee and Ezo large bumble bee queens would still end up laying eggs, but they wouldn't hatch. This means no new bees to replace the existing ones that would

FIGURE 4-2. *Bombus hypocrita hypocrita*, the large bumble bee.

FIGURE 4-3. *Bombus hypocrita sapporoensis*, the Ezo large bumble bee.

eventually die off. If this happened enough times, it would spell disaster for the populations of these two wild bumble bees.

---

1.   Ezo means the north island of Japan, where this bee is found.

Another research group discovered that as buff-tailed bumble bees were expanding their range (the region where they live) across northern Japan, they were creating·competition for nesting sites with native bumble bee species. Competition was so fierce that the population of native bumble bee species was falling. The scientists even warned of local extinction: The species might die out and no longer exist.

The evidence also showed that buff-tailed bumble bees might threaten the natural pollination systems already established in the environment. In a clever experiment, scientists gathered seven different native plants and presented them to bumble bees in three separate greenhouses. The first greenhouse had only native bumble bee species, the second greenhouse had only buff-tailed bumble bees, and the third greenhouse had a mix of both native species of bumble bees and buff-tails. So, in a way, the first greenhouse represented a situation where buff-tailed bumble bees had not been introduced into the environment at all. The second greenhouse represented the possibility of buff-tails completely taking over from native pollinators; and the third greenhouse mimicked a situation where buff-tailed bumble bees were initially introduced into the natural environment and were sharing territory with native pollinators, but had not yet pushed them out.

The scientists gave the bumble bees in each greenhouse time to visit the seven different species of native flowers.

After the flowers grew fruit, the scientists compared the quality of the fruit between the different greenhouses. The greenhouse with just the native bumble bee species produced the best fruit. Fruit that came from the greenhouse with only buff-tailed bumble bees produced fruit that was much smaller and weighed less, indicating that the buff-tailed individuals did not do as good a job of pollinating the native plants compared to the native species of bumble bees. Interestingly, the greenhouse that had a mix of both native bumble bee species and buff-tails did not produce fruit that was of "medium" quality, as you might expect. Instead, the fruit quality was rather unpredictable. What does all of this mean? Introducing a new bumble bee species into the wild can greatly change the pollination of native plants, affecting the fruit of the plants and the survival of the plants as a whole—even if the population of the newly introduced bumble bee species is initially not very large.

Finally, researchers had warned that importing commercial bumble bee colonies would introduce new diseases and infections to native bumble bee species. A Japanese research group indeed found *tracheal mites* in some buff-tailed worker bumble bees from colonies that were imported from Europe. Tracheal mites are very tiny creatures that live in the trachea of bumble bees: the tubes in their respiratory system that deliver air to their cells. Little is known about the mite, other than it pierces bumble bees' trachea and eats their blood. If these mites infest a colony, they can cause diarrhea and make some bumble bees too tired to forage. Because the mite was brought over from Europe, and thus is foreign to Japan, it is unknown what effect the mites will have on the population of native Japanese bumble bees if they spread into the wild.

Japan did eventually take steps to try to avoid or lessen the impact of importing buff-tailed bumble bees. The country began to commercialize one of its own species of bumble bee, what is known in Japan as the black bumble bee (*Bombus ignitus*). That way greenhouses could use a native species of bumble bee to pollinate crops. If there were escapees that established nests in the wild, this would not threaten the natural population of black bumble bees. In fact, it might even strengthen it.

FIGURE 4-4. The black bumble bee (*Bombus ignitus*), with a big ball of pollen on her back leg.

Still, there were some problems. Some colonies of black bumble bees were mass-produced in Japan, but many queens of that species were captured in the wild and shipped to bumble bee breeding facilities in the Netherlands. Then they were shipped back to Japan to be used for pollination. But all was not well. A group of Japanese researchers soon found that the colonies that were coming back from the Netherlands contained the tracheal mite.

There are over one hundred known bee parasites in the wild, including viruses, fungi, mites, and nematodes. Parasites that are specific to certain areas of the world can be found in that area's native bumble bee species. Often these parasites pose no noticeable threat to the bees, and it is thought that the native bumble bees are somewhat immune to the parasites. However, introduce a parasite from one country to a population of bumble bees thousands of miles away, and there is no way to predict the effect it may have. For example, Japanese scientists found that their native large bumble bee and Ezo large bumble bee populations carried a type of tracheal mite that had different genes from the one found in Europe. The scientists warned that if people started to ship the large bumble bee and Ezo large bumble bee to the Netherlands to be mass-produced like black bumble bees, there was the very real possibility that this type of mite could infect European bumble bees. There was no predicting what effect such an infestation would have.

The bottom line is that shipping bumble bee colonies—whether they are foreign or native species of bumble bees—poses the risk of an infestation by parasites, both in commercial and natural bumble bee colonies.

Scientists urged that companies establish some type of quarantine system for commercial bumble bee colonies.

But Japan wasn't the only place where commercial buff-tailed bumble bees were causing big problems. On the other side of the globe, they were posing a huge threat to none other than the biggest bumble bee in the world.

CHILE & ARGENTINA

In the forests at the southern tip of South America lives "a monstrous fluffy ginger beast."[2] This "beast" is *Bombus dahlbomii*: the world's largest bumble bee.

As we saw in Chapter Two, in Argentina this bee is commonly known as *Manganga*, and in Chile it

FIGURE 4-5. The giant ginger bumble bee (*Bombus dahlbomii*).

is referred to as *Moscardón*. In this book we'll refer to it as the giant ginger bumble bee. It is thought to be the only native bumble bee species in this area of the planet, which encompasses southern Argentina and Chile, also known as the Patagonia region of South America.

---

2.   This description was coined by Dr. Dave Goulson, a renowned bumble bee scientist in the United Kingdom.

The giant ginger bumble bee buzzes from flower to flower, pollinating a variety of different forest plants. One of these plants is the Peruvian lily (*Alstroemeria aurea*). It is a wild lily that is related to a number of types of lilies that are sold in flower shops across the globe. The giant ginger bumble bee, the Peruvian lily, and the rest of the forest flora enjoyed a very peaceful and mutually beneficial relationship: The flowers

FIGURE 4-6. Map of Patagonia in South America.

ers provided the gentle giant with pollen and nectar for food, and the bees pollinated the flowers, ensuring that the plants continued to prosper.

As we saw in Chapter One, people introduced a group of ruderal bumble bee queens into Chile in the 1980s, and this species of bumble bee soon established colonies in the wild and spread into Argentina. Then, in 1998, commercial buff-tailed bumble bee colonies were imported from Europe to Chile to pollinate tomatoes. By 2006, buff-tails were spotted in the Patagonia region, and it was estimated that they had spread approximately 124 miles per year from the original release site!

The giant ginger bumble bee now had two other bumble bee species to contend with: the ruderal bumble bee and the buff-tailed bumble bee. Would there be any effects?

Word began to spread that the giant ginger bumble bee was being seen less and less in its homeland. To determine whether the talk was true, a group of scien-

FIGURE 4-7. The Peruvian lily (*Alstroemeria aurea*).

tists decided to conduct a large-scale bumble bee survey of the Patagonia region, along with a twenty-year study of which bumble bee species visited wild Peruvian lilies. What they found was shocking.

At the beginning of the twenty-year study of Peruvian lily visitors, which was in 1994, approximately 95 percent of the visitors to the flowers were the giant ginger bumble bee. Ruderal bumble bees, the new bees on the block, accounted for only about 1 percent of the visits. So, it appeared that the giant ginger bumble bee was still the main pollinator of the Peruvian lily, and ruderal bumble bees were not giving it much competition. (The remaining 4 percent of visitors consisted of native flies, beetles, butterflies, solitary bees, and hummingbirds.) However, after 2008, no giant ginger bumble bees were seen visiting any Peruvian lilies. Ruderal bumble bees, and to an even larger extent, the additional newcomer the buff-tailed bumble bee, were taking over. This takeover was made even more evident by the survey results. Over 29 years, ruderal bumble bees spread about 270 miles beyond their 1982 release sites. In half that time, buff-tailed bumble bees spread approximately 820 miles from where they were released!

Buff-tails were also by far the most abundant bumble bee species observed in the areas the scientists included in their study. In fact, they found that wherever buff-tails had established colonies, the giant ginger bumble bee disappeared completely. Their evidence strongly suggests that buff-tailed bumble bees displaced the native giant ginger bumble bee. It has now gotten to the point where this large, lovable bumble bee species is considered at risk of extinction. Curiously, ruderal bumble bees carry on, and they don't seem anywhere near as affected by the buff-tail invasion.

But what exactly is causing the mass disappearance of the giant ginger bumble bee? The decline has happened too fast to be due to flower or nest site competition with buff-tailed bumble bees. The leading suspects so far are parasites.

Two parasites in particular, *Crithidia bombi* and *Apicystis bombi* (we'll call them *C. bombi* and *A. bombi* for short), are believed to have been transported by ruderal and buff-tailed newcomers into Argentina. *C. bombi* lives in the intestines of bumble bees and is too small to see with the naked eye. It spreads when bumble bees come into contact with contaminated parts of the nest or if they drink from flowers with contaminated nectar. *C. bombi* is often found in buff-tailed bumble bees, and it doesn't seem to bother them. However, this parasite can kill the bee if it is unable to get enough food, and some scientists found that a high intensity of infection with this parasite can interfere with a bee's ability to learn how to get nectar and pollen from flowers.

A. bombi, the other parasite, lives in the fat body of bumble bees and other insects. The fat body is a loose piece of flesh found inside an insect. It is important for regulating how the insect's cells burn energy, it allows the insect to fend off illness and disease, and it stores energy when food is scarce. Some scientists found that when infected with *A. bombi*, bumble bees had a much lower fat content and some bees even died. A lower fat content is dangerous for bumble bees: It makes them more vulnerable to diseases, and they are less likely to survive during times when nectar stores in the nest are low and they are unable to forage, for instance, during days of stormy weather. Low fat content is especially dangerous for queen bumble bees, as they rely on fat stores to provide them with energy during hibernation. If a queen bumble bee does not have enough fat stored in her fat body, she may not survive the winter. If she dies, then there will be no new bumble bee colony in the spring.

A group of scientists captured a number of giant ginger bumble bees both before and after buff-tailed bumble bees invaded the Patagonia region. They examined them for any evidence of *A. bombi* infection. Indeed, they found that *A. bombi* was present in the giant, rusty-colored bumble bee species, but only in bees that were sampled after buff-tails had come to the area. This strongly suggests that buff-tailed bumble bees introduced the parasite to South America, and it spilled over into the population of the native giant ginger bumble bee.

As far as we know, the parasites *C. bombi* and *A. bombi* did not exist previously in South America. Having never been exposed to these parasites before, giant ginger bumble bees would not have had a chance to develop immunity against them. These bees might therefore be more sensitive to the effects of the new parasites. What might not kill buff-tailed bumble bees (what we call sublethal effects, as we learned earlier) could spell doom for the giant ginger bumble bee.

Are *C. bombi* and *A. bombi* infecting Patagonia's gentle giant and causing these bees to die? Whatever the cause may be, no one could have predicted the aggressive spread of buff-tailed bumble bees and the devastation to the giant ginger bumble bee.

ESCAPEE #2: THE COMMON EASTERN BUMBLE BEE

CANADA & THE UNITED STATES

FIGURE 4-8. A partial map of North America showing the location of Newfoundland and Labrador.

The province of Newfoundland and Labrador is located on the most eastern tip of Canada. Labrador is the name given to the mainland portion of the province, whereas Newfoundland is the name of the small nearby island.

Compared to other Canadian provinces, the total number of bee species in Newfoundland is quite small. So far, only 74 bee species have been recorded there, whereas in the mainland province of Nova Scotia, for example, 217 species have been recorded. Of the seventy-four bee species in Newfoundland, there are about nine species of bumble bees. We're not sure of the status of these bumble bee populations. Are they healthy? Or are they in danger of dying out? Not enough research has been done yet. However, bumble bees in Newfoundland have not experienced the same kinds of stresses that bumble bees from other provinces have faced and that have been linked to population declines, namely the use of pesticides on farmland and the loss of natural land when cities are built or expanded. Also, being an island, Newfoundland is rather isolated from any diseases that may be infecting bumble bees on the mainland.

In North America, the main bumble bee species that is raised commercially is the common eastern bumble bee, which is native to parts of Canada and the United States. (Buff-tailed bumble bees are not allowed to be imported into those two countries.) So, farmers in Newfoundland had been adding boxes of commercial common eastern bumble bees to their blueberries and cranberries, with the hope that the extra bumble bees would result in more and/or plumper fruit.

Although the common eastern bumble bee is native to some parts of North America, it is *not* native to Newfoundland. And Dr. Barry Hicks, who works at Memorial University in Newfoundland, questioned whether importing bumble bees—and an exotic bumble bee species at that—was necessary, given the populations of native bees on the island, and given that wild blueberries had been doing just fine for years.

Dr. Hicks and his team compared farmland in which plots of blueberry or cranberry plants were given commercial bumble bees with areas of plants that had no commercial bumble bees (and were thus pollinated by native bees). They found no benefit to using commercial bumble bees: They did not produce any more fruit, and they did not produce better quality fruit. This meant that farmers might be getting no benefit from purchasing and using commercial bumble bees at all—they might as well have relied on the natural pollination job done by wild bees.

But the team also noticed something disturbing. When Dr. Hicks and his team looked inside the boxes of commercial bumble bees, they found a number of wild species! For some reason, individuals of the orange-belted bumble bee or tricolored bumble bee (*Bombus ternarius*), the half-black bumble bee (*Bombus vagans bolsteri*), the frigid bumble bee (*Bombus frigidus*), and the yellow-banded bumble bee (*Bombus terricola*) had "drifted" into the commercial nests. Perhaps they were trying to steal some of the stored nectar? Drifting bumble bees stealing nectar has been known to happen in the wild, and even between commercial bumble bee colonies in greenhouses. What was very concerning, though, was that if there were any diseases in the commercial nests, they could spread to these wild "drifters," who could then bring the disease back to their home nests, thereby spreading the disease into the wild. Indeed, when the researchers screened the commercial colonies for seven possible diseases, they tested positive for three.

The use of commercial bumble bee colonies to pollinate blueberries and cranberries is very dangerous for another reason, too. Blueberries and cranberries are grown in open fields or farmland; they are not contained within a structure such as a greenhouse. So, when the boxes of commercial bumble bees are opened and placed in these areas, the bumble bees are free to fly anywhere. This includes any male bumble bees or new queens that hatch near the end of the colony life cycle. These bees would then be free to start establishing a population of common eastern bumble bees in the wild. If this happens, will they create competition for nesting sites and food with the native Newfoundland bumble bee species? Would they cause the wild species to decline, and/or breed with the wild species to create hybrids?

Thanks to Dr. Hicks's research, the government of Newfoundland and Labrador has since banned farmers from importing commercial colonies of common eastern bumble bees—and any other species of bees for that matter. But have diseases from past imports spread to native populations of bumble bees? We simply do not know.

And unfortunately, laws don't stop everyone. A few years ago, a farmer in Newfoundland illegally imported colonies of common eastern bumble bees that had already been used by farmers in New Brunswick, a neighboring Canadian province. "The government actually confiscated the boxes of bees from the farmer's fields," Dr. Hicks said. But even so, some common eastern bumble bee queens were found in the wild the following spring: They had emerged from hibernation to start their own colonies, after mating in the preceding summer. This was a sign that the species had made a home in Newfoundland. Luckily, Dr. Hicks and his team searched all around the farm the spring after that, and didn't find any new common eastern queens. "We dodged a bullet," said Dr. Hicks.

The common eastern bumble bee might not have established itself in Newfoundland, but the same cannot be said for the more western provinces of Canada, or for the western United States. As its name implies, this species of bumble bee is naturally found in the more eastern parts of Canada and the United States. It has been produced commercially for farmers in the eastern parts of those countries, since breeding a native species of bumble bee seemed to be a smart thing to do: If any bees escaped from greenhouses or were set free to forage in the fields, they would only be enhancing the abundance of a naturally occurring species in the area.

But the western part of Canada and the United States

have crops to pollinate, too. For a while, using the same logic of breeding a native species, commercial companies supplied colonies of the western bumble bee (*Bombus occidentalis*) to western farmers.

FIGURE 4-9. The western bumble bee (*Bombus occidentalis*).

Unfortunately, in the late 1990s, there was a terrible outbreak of an intestinal fungus-type parasite, *Nosema bombi* (we'll call it *N. bombi* for short), which led to the collapse of the commercial population of the western bumble bee. (When a population of bees collapses, it means that many or most of the individuals of that species disappear, become ill, or die.) The wild population collapsed, too. It is still a mystery why the western bumble bee is so vulnerable to *N. bombi*. In any event, commercial bumble bee companies stopped breeding that species.[3] That left western farmers high and dry without bumble bees to pollinate their vast areas of crops! So, in 1999, an emergency program was started that allowed farmers in British Columbia and Alberta, Canada, to import

---

3.   Thankfully, some individuals of the western bumble bee managed to survive, and this species can still be found in the wild. However, this bumble bee is still considered vulnerable to extinction.

colonies of the common eastern bumble bee from the east. There were conditions, however: Farmers had to destroy all colonies by the end of the program (which was November of 1999), and they needed to use queen excluders to prevent queen bumble bees from escaping.[4]

After the emergency program ended, in 2000, the Canadian and United States governments stopped managing imports of bumble bee colonies between provinces (in the case of Canada) and between states (in the case of the United States). They pretty much left it up to the individual provinces and states whether they wanted to impose any rules about the importation of the common eastern bumble bee. So, most provinces and states allowed this species of bee to continue to be imported for both greenhouse and open field pollination, likely because they believed that adding bees to food crops would result in more and/or better pollination (and therefore better quality food) compared to what native or wild bees already did on their own. Also, at the time, the common eastern bumble bee was the only species of bumble bee that was being sold in those two countries.

However, some scientists weren't convinced that it was a good idea to continue to import the common eastern bumble bee into western provinces and states. In 2003, a group

---

4. Queen excluders are special "doors" fitted into the colony box that are big enough to allow workers to pass through but are too small for queens.

FIGURE 4-10. World map showing the location of the Canadian province of British Columbia, in black and circled.

of scientists counted the number of bee species in strawberry fields near Vancouver, British Columbia. These fields were two to three miles from the nearest greenhouses, where commercial common eastern bumble bees would have been kept. But they found several common eastern worker bees and a queen: evidence that this imported species of bumble bee might now live in the wild in British Columbia.

Since then, the common eastern bumble bee is now widespread in southwestern British Columbia, and it lives in the wild in Washington State. Scientists predict that the species will likely continue to spread into California, and it has already spread into the neighboring province of Alberta, Canada. What will be the effects of this eastern bumble bee species on western ecosystems? Only time will tell.

IMPORTING MORE THAN JUST BUMBLE BEES

One of the biggest worries about shipping bumble bees remains their ability to carry diseases into new places. Up until the year 2008, there were several reports of commercial bumble bee colonies carrying pathogens. As a result, many countries began to require mandatory disease screening of colonies before they could be imported. The companies that produced the colonies began to claim that their colonies were pathogen-free.

Still, some bumble bee scientists were skeptical. In 2011 and 2012, one research group in England decided to take a close look at some commercial colonies. They purchased a number of colonies of buff-tailed bumble bees from three different companies. With apparently healthy bumble bee colonies in hand, the scientists set to work to test whether the colonies were in fact pathogen-free.

Their results were stunning. Out of forty-eight bumble bee colonies, only eleven colonies were free of pathogens (23 percent). Parasites were found in bees from all three companies. Some of the pathogens could be transmitted to other bumble bees simply by contact with the same flower surfaces. If these commercial bumble bees escaped from greenhouses and foraged in the wild, they could spread their diseases to other bees by contaminating flowers that the other bees would visit. Some of the pathogens that were found in the commercial bumble bees could even infect honey bees.

The researchers ran tests to confirm that the pathogens would make other bees sick. They exposed healthy, disease-free bumble bees and honey bees to the pathogens taken from the commercial colonies. When the disease-free bumble bees and honey bees did become infected, a number of the bees died. This meant that the pathogens that these supposedly "pathogen-free" commercial bumble bees carried were contagious—to bumble bees as well as honey bees—and ultimately deadly.

The final blow came when the scientists also analyzed the pollen that had been shipped with the commercial colonies. Pollen, often from honey bees, is placed in commercial bumble bee colonies to be used as food for baby bees until the colonies reach their destination and can go looking for pollen on their own. Out of the twenty-five pollen samples that the scientists took, only one sample was free of every pathogen that they screened for. When they fed the contaminated pollen to healthy bumble bee and honey bee adults (by mixing it with sugar and water), the bees became sick and died. They also fed the contaminated pollen to honey bee larvae, and they did not survive either.

Whatever methods the commercial bumble bee companies were using to screen their colonies for disease before shipping were obviously not working. At the time, the United Kingdom was importing approximately forty thousand to fifty thousand bumble bee colonies per year. If the study that the scientists conducted truly reflected the state of commercial colonies, then roughly 77 percent of all of those colonies—over thirty thousand each year—had the potential to spread deadly diseases to bumble bee and honey bee populations.

Unfortunately, the situation was not unique to the United Kingdom. In 2006, a study came out from Canadian researchers who investigated whether pathogens could spread from a heavily infected group of animals (in this case, commercial bumble bees) to a non-infected group (wild bumble bees). We call this pathogen spillover. Wild bumble bees were thought to become infected by sharing flowers that had been visited by escaped commercial bumble bees, or by escaped commercial bumble bees who entered the nests of wild bumble bees.

The researchers caught a large number of bumble bees from six different locations in southern Ontario: Three locations were near at least one commercial greenhouse, and three locations were far away from any commercial greenhouses. If pathogen spillover was happening between commercial and wild bumble bees, then the bumble bees that were caught near greenhouses would show more infection by pathogens compared to bumble bees that were caught far away from greenhouses. This is exactly what they found. The intestinal parasite *C. bombi* was found in a number of bumble bees that were captured near greenhouses, but it was totally absent in bumble bees caught far away from greenhouses. Another intestinal parasite, *N. bombi*, was three times more likely to be found in bumble bees near greenhouses compared to the other sites.

It's possible that some of the bumble bees that were caught during the study were not wild bumble bees at all but were in fact greenhouse escapees. However, the researchers tracked the species of bumble bees that they caught, and the common eastern bumble bee—commercial or wild—made up only a third of the total 628 bumble bees that were captured. The rest of the bumble bees in their sample were a number of different species that are found in the wild. So, the majority of the captured bumble bees were from the wild, and indeed a number of these wild bees carried *C. bombi* or *N. bombi*. All signs were that pathogen spillover from commercial to wild bumble bees was occurring.

Far away in Mexico, thousands of commercial colonies of the common eastern bumble bee enter the country every year. In 2008, seven thousand colonies were imported, and in 2007, twenty-four thousand were imported. As with any other country that uses a large number of commercial bumble bee colonies, there are definitely escapees. But are these common eastern bumble bee colonies healthy? Or do they carry pathogens that could spread out into the surrounding ecosystem? A group of scientists in Mexico decided to find out.

The study began with 120 commercial colonies of common eastern bumble bees that were donated by 120 different greenhouses. The scientists took ten worker bees from each colony and ran a number of screening tests for ten different bee pathogens. The results were not reassuring. Out of 120 colonies, 54 (45 percent) tested positive for one or more pathogens. Some of the bumble bees were infected by one or more of the viruses that have been associated with colony collapse disorder in honey bees (we'll see much more about colony collapse disorder in Chapter Five). But the kicker of this study? It was published in 2015. Years had passed since research started to show that commercial bumble bee colonies were carrying disease, and yet still not enough was being done. Wild bumble bee populations were still being put at risk with each colony shipment—possibly millions of them every year.

HOW SHOULD WE DEAL WITH INVASIVE BUMBLE BEES?

We must remember why bumble bee colonies are being produced and shipped by the thousands each year: to pollinate crops that provide us with the food we eat. Tomatoes, sweet peppers, blueberries, and a number of other fruits and vegetables that humans eat in huge amounts are pollinated by bumble bees. Bumble bees do us a great service. They help plants grow. They are small, charming, diligent hard workers that mind their own business in getting food to their bumble bee families. You can see why people don't think of them as threats to the environment.

And after seeing the evidence of the harm commercial bumble bees can do to wild pollinators, it is easy to see commercial bumble bee producers as the bad guys. However, their intentions are to run a successful business, to fill a need, and to help bring food to our tables. Their goal is certainly not to destroy the environment. The same major companies that sell bumble bee colonies also provide a number of biological, "environmentally friendly" methods of pest control to serve as alternatives to using harmful pesticides. Their bumble bee nest boxes come equipped with queen excluders to help keep their colonies contained.

As we have seen, commercial bumble bees escaping from greenhouses into the wild can have major effects on the surrounding environment. They can establish colonies in the wild, potentially push out native bumble bee species and other pollinators, and pollinate (and thereby spread) invasive plant species.[5]

But the biggest threat of all is the spread of pathogens and disease. The large, factory-like conditions in which commercial bumble bees are raised are perfect breeding

---

5. *Invasive* refers to a new plant or animal that is introduced to an area. It has no predators to control its population. It spreads quickly and widely, and is harmful to the native species of an area.

grounds for pathogens. We need to use better methods to screen commercial colonies for illnesses both while they are in the factory before they are shipped, and once they arrive at their destination. Even after shipping, the bees can suffer from a phenomenon called shipping fever. Shipping fever happens when the stress from traveling lowers an animal's resistance to parasites and disease. And we should not only be screening the bumble bees, but screening for the honey bee pollen that is fed to them as they are shipped from one place to another.

The tricky part is that bumble bees can carry parasites and disease without showing any visible symptoms. There are laboratory analyses that the bee-producing companies can do to screen bumble bees, but putting these steps into practice would take extra time, money, and resources. Are companies willing to invest in stricter screening processes? Will they test the honey bee pollen for risks as well? And more importantly, should stricter screening processes become law?

And what can we do to stop commercially produced bumble bees from escaping from greenhouses? The challenge is that greenhouses need ventilation. They need open windows and/or vents leading to the outside. In Japan, it is now the law to have screens or netting over greenhouse windows and vents. But is this enough? There will always be doors opening, broken windows or cracks, netting or screens that become loose . . . Considering how small bumble bees are, they don't need very big spaces to slip through.

What about the farmers? What should they do with all of their commercial bumble bee colonies once the life cycle of each colony comes to an end and they are left with a bunch of new queens and males? How should farmers properly dispose of the colonies, so that the new queens and males don't escape into the wild? And how can proper disposal of colonies be enforced?

The story of the giant ginger bumble bee in Patagonia serves as a warning for what could happen when imported, non-native bumble bee species escape from their commercial colonies and become established in the wild. This beautiful big bumble bee is now endangered. Its habitat has been taken over by the buff-tailed bumble bee. We don't yet know what effects buff-tails are also having on Patagonian plants, or on other native pollinators. And remember, bumble bees are oblivious to borders: Argentina never imported buff-tailed bumble bees, but it has to contend with an invasion from neighboring Chile. A similar situation is occurring between the province of British Columbia and the state of Washington with the common eastern bumble bee.

If only there was a way to round up and remove all the buff-tailed bumble bees (and common eastern bumble bees, in the case of North America) that have escaped and established themselves in foreign lands. This would prevent the endangerment of native species such as the giant ginger bumble bee and protect the overall natural balance of the ecosystem. But being so small and so numerous, and given that their nests are hard to find, this task seems virtually impossible. And where would we put all the captured bees? Or would we destroy them? One recent report from Japan recommended spraying a pesticide on buff-tailed worker bees that are found out in the open, particularly in two Japanese national parks. The particular pesticide that the scientists have in mind is called an insect growth regulator. It does not seem to kill adult bumble bees, but by spraying adult bees, they would carry the pesticide back to their nests, where it would kill eggs, larvae, and pupae. So, the pesticide would prevent new buff-tailed bumble bees from emerging and the adult population would eventually die off.

As we will see in later chapters, humans have used pesticides this way before to kill insect pests, but they do serious harm to beneficial insects, such as bees. These pesticides have also gotten into soil and water, and we are only beginning to realize the impact this is having on the environment. How can we be 100 percent certain that the pesticide that is used to control buff-tailed bumble bees will not affect other species, especially if it is sprayed in parks with wild animals ranging from insects to amphibians to mammals? Would it affect plants, soil, and/or water? Scientists may have tested, and possibly ruled out, short-term effects of the pesticide, but what about long-term effects? How do we know that the pesticide doesn't have a delayed effect on animals, plants, and the surrounding environment as a whole?[6]

To truly solve the problem of invasive species, we need to strike some kind of balance between the needs of humans and the protection of natural ecosystems. A number of expert groups have recommended that local species of bumble bees be commercially produced in areas where they are found in the wild, instead of importing foreign species from other countries or from other provinces or states. This way, any escapees would only be enhancing the native population of bumble bees. Also, any parasites or pathogens carried by the escapees would likely already exist in that area, with native bumble bee species having developed a resistance to them. As a precaution, given that factory-like conditions are breeding grounds for illness and disease, we would also screen commercial colonies, both before and after they were shipped to their destination. This strategy requires commercial bumble bee companies, and those who use commercial colonies, to make major changes to how they do business. In addition, governments and science-funding organizations must invest resources into studying bumble bee pathogens and how to detect

6.   There is a concept called *bioaccumulation*, which happens when there is a build-up of a toxic substance over time in an animal.

them. With the existence of entire species and the general health of the environment at stake, these changes and investments have to become our responsibility.

No one could have predicted that selling bumble bees around the world to pollinate food crops would result in the spread of disease and a threat to wild bee species. The intentions were good, but the result has been potentially environmentally catastrophic! And no one could have predicted this next major event: the mysterious disappearance of millions of honey bees.

CHAPTER FIVE

Bees in the Spotlight

EMPTY HIVES

It was 2006. Reports trickled in from the East Coast of the United States that commercial honey bee keepers had lost an "alarming" number of their honey bee colonies.[1] By the end of the year, honey bee keepers from the West Coast were complaining about the same thing. It was like a plot from a mystery novel: Beekeepers would open up their hives to find that almost all of the thousands of adult honey bees were gone, leaving behind all of the eggs, larvae, and immature bees, plus multiple pounds of stored honey. The honey bees had just flown away, and they never came back. Why

---

1. Commercial honey bee keepers rent their numerous hives to farmers so the bees can pollinate their crops. Often this involves shipping the beehives great distances across the country.

did they leave? Where did they go? They might have left their hives to die, but dead honey bee bodies were never found. In fact, there were no traces of the lost honey bees anywhere. They had completely disappeared.

By the end of winter 2007, the number of commercial honey bee colonies in the United States was estimated to have dropped 31.8 percent. Individual beekeepers reported that they lost between 30 percent and 90 percent of their colonies. The mysterious honey bee disappearances continued into 2007 and 2008, and losses were higher, at 35.8 percent. By that point honey bee keepers from Canada, Europe, South and Central America, and Asia were also complaining of disappearing honey bees. More than a decade later, it's still an ongoing problem.

Should we be worried? Annual honey bee colony losses are not uncommon. Beekeepers usually lose about 10 percent of their colonies each spring due to a number of reasons, including bee pests, parasites, pathogens, and disease. And, looking at the situation long-term, beekeepers tend to suffer unusually heavy colony losses about once every ten years. As far back as the year 950, there are reports of a "great mortality of bees" in Ireland, which happened again in 992 and in 1443. One of the most famous honey bee catastrophes occurred in 1906, when most beekeepers in the Isle of Wight in the United Kingdom lost all of their colonies. In Colorado in 1891 and 1896, beekeepers witnessed the disappearance of large clusters of honey bees over a short period of time. They called the condition May Disease. In 1903, in the Cache Valley of Utah, two thousand colonies perished; and more recently, in 1995, Pennsylvania beekeepers lost 53 percent of their colonies. However, the mysterious disappearance of honey bees in 2006 and 2007 was different. It occurred suddenly across a number of states and countries, and many beekeepers lost most of their hives. This was definitely at the extreme end of the continuum of honey bee losses.

THE MYSTERY NAMED

In the past when a large number of honey bee colonies died in the spring due to a lack of adult bees, people called it disappearing disease or spring dwindling. So at first, the losses of 2006 and 2007 were referred to as Fall-Dwindle Disease. But that name was not quite accurate. The mysterious honey bee disappearances happened not only in the fall but throughout the year. The word *dwindle* suggests a gradual disappearance, whereas bees were vanishing very suddenly. *Disease* implies that we know what the cause is, but no cause had been found. The term *disappearance* was already used to describe past situations that didn't quite fit the latest losses. Eventually, researchers and beekeepers settled on the name *colony collapse disorder*, or CCD.

There are specific symptoms associated with CCD, which sets it apart from other kinds of honey bee losses. The key signs are that most or all of the adult population of honey bees in a hive disappear, with no trace of dead bees. What is left behind in the hive are the *brood* (immature bees), the pollen and honey stores, and the queen bee, sometimes with a small cluster of worker bees. Often the queen bee continues to lay eggs, but there are nowhere near enough adult worker bees to help look after the brood. The remaining cluster of bees tends not to eat the food provided by the beekeeper and also rarely forages. Honey bee colonies afflicted with CCD are pretty much doomed.

The fact that so many honey bees were completely abandoning their hives is incredibly strange. Honey bees are extremely social and belong to colonies that are complex and highly organized. Helping their colony succeed, whether by foraging outside for food, caring for the brood, or keeping the nest clean, is a honey bee's top priority. Abandoning their family was a signal that something had gone terribly wrong.

The lack of dead bees made it difficult to pinpoint a cause for CCD because scientists couldn't study any of them for clues. There was no evidence that hives were attacked by some sort of predator. Given the importance of honey bees to our food systems, the United States government prioritized investigating CCD.

At the time of the honey bee losses in 2006 and 2007, the US Department of Agriculture recorded about 2,800 beekeeping operations with a total of almost three million honey bee colonies across the United States. Although these operations produce honey for sale, their value is mostly in the pollination services they provide to food crops. Each year, US farmers rent more than two million honey bee colonies. About half of these colonies are sent to California to pollinate thousands of acres of almond trees, as almonds rely almost exclusively on honey bees for pollination. Other crops that are almost completely dependent on honey bee pollination include apples, avocados, cherries, kiwi fruit, macadamia nuts, asparagus, broccoli, carrots, cauliflower, celery, cucumbers, onions, pumpkins, squash, and sunflowers. If CCD puts honey bees in jeopardy, all of these foods we eat are in jeopardy, too.

And if that wasn't enough, some researchers warned that the number of available commercial honey bee colonies was not keeping pace with growing demand for pollination: More people living and being born in the United States means more demand for food, which means more need for bees to pollinate more crops. The United States could not afford to lose honey bees to CCD.

Between 2007 and 2010, the United States government provided over $31 million for research into honey bee health and CCD. But would this investment help researchers and beekeepers get to the bottom of the puzzle?

INVESTIGATING THE MYSTERY OF CCD

Researchers from the United States government and universities quickly teamed up and launched studies to investigate CCD. The government also established the Bee Research Laboratory in Beltsville, Maryland, whose focus is to improve the health of honey bees and help maintain an adequate supply of commercial honey bee colonies for pollinating crops.

In one particular project, honey bee experts from the Bee Research Laboratory teamed up with experts from American and Belgian universities and set out to compare honey bee colonies that had been afflicted with CCD with colonies that had not. They chose ninety-one colonies across thirteen apiaries (places where people keep honey bee hives) in Florida and California. The researchers classified the apiaries into one of two categories: (1) apiaries having no colonies with CCD symptoms (this was referred to as the "control" group); or (2) apiaries having colonies with CCD symptoms (referred to as the "CCD" group). In order to be in the CCD group, the apiaries must have experienced a rapid loss of adult worker bees so that colonies were either dead or very weak, such that there were not enough worker bees to look after the brood. They would have found no dead bees either within or surrounding the hives. Also, honey bees or other animals, such as small hive beetles or wax moths, could not have robbed the abandoned hives of their ample supplies of stored pollen and honey.[2]

Once the apiaries were categorized as being in either the CCD or the control group, the scientists took samples of adult honey bees and froze them on ice. (In hives that experienced CCD, they collected whatever few worker bees remained.) They also took samples of the hives' comb, which contained wax and sometimes (but not always) immature bees. The frozen honey bees, wax, and immature bees were sent to a lab for analysis. The scientists hoped that by comparing the bees, wax, and immature bees between apiaries that had suffered CCD with those that had not, there would be clear differences that pointed to the possible cause(s) of CCD.

The research team tested for sixty-one different measurements between the two groups. These included physical measurements (for example, body mass of the bees and body protein content); measurements for viruses, bacteria, and parasites; and measurements for pesticide residues. Surely by testing for such a large number of possible causes of CCD the researchers would uncover the secret behind the disappearing honey bees.

But then the results came in. Not one measure was

---

2.   This symptom of CCD was also quite strange. The fact that other animals weren't stealing all of the pollen and honey left behind from CCD colonies was another sign that something was very wrong.

obviously different between the CCD and control colonies. In fact, no one factor was found consistently and in great enough amounts in the CCD colonies to suggest a single cause for CCD. But the researchers did uncover three clues. When they looked at the arrangement of the honey bee colonies in the apiaries, they noticed that apiaries that suffered from CCD had more dead or weak colonies, and these dead or weak colonies were much more likely to be next to each other. This suggests that whatever causes CCD is contagious, or that CCD colonies are exposed to the same risk factor.

Another clue was that compared to control colonies, CCD colonies tended to have higher virus levels and were infected with many more disease agents. So, although there might not be one specific pathogen causing CCD, pathogens do seem to play a key role.

Control colonies also contained higher concentrations of *coumaphos*. Coumaphos is a product used by beekeepers to control the mite *Varroa destructor.* Varroa mites are tiny, reddish-colored, disc-shaped parasites that latch onto honey bees and suck out their blood. (For that reason, varroa mites are also called vampire mites.) Vampire mites are known to weaken the honey bee immune system and give viruses to the bees. If control colonies had a higher concentration of these mites, their beekeepers probably controlled for vampire mites more aggressively than beekeepers of

CCD-afflicted apiaries. That would explain the higher concentrations of coumaphos. Curiously, vampire mite levels was one of the sixty-one measurements that the scientists compared between CCD and control colonies. Since there was no difference in mite levels between the CCD and control colonies, the mites by themselves could not be the sole cause of CCD. However, could there have been a difference in vampire mite levels before the scientists took their samples? Or perhaps there was a difference in mite levels before the beekeepers treated the colonies? It was another puzzle. More research would have to be done before vampire mite infestations could be completely ruled out as a contributor to CCD.

The thing is, as the researchers point out in their report, they assumed that whatever causes CCD was still hanging around when they collected their honey bee and wax samples. But that might not be true. For example, if pollen contaminated with pesticides actually causes CCD, this pollen would have been eaten by bees, these bees would have disappeared, and then the contaminated pollen would not have been in the nest to be sampled as part of their study. Or, if there is a particular disease that causes CCD, the diseased bees would have disappeared before the scientists gathered their samples, so the disease would not be detected in the ones left behind.

In the end, this research team did not solve the mystery

of CCD. However, like any good scientific study, their results suggested places that others could do more research. It was clear that the honey bees from CCD apiaries were "sicker" than the honey bees from control apiaries: They had a higher level of pathogens and were infected with more than one pathogen. Are bees affected by CCD exposed to higher levels of pathogens? Or is CCD at least partially caused by a weakened honey bee immune system?

The scientists were also suspicious of the role of vampire mites in CCD. And even though they tested for differences in pesticide residues between the CCD and control bees, and found no differences, they felt they could not rule out pesticides as a possible contributor to CCD with certainty. What if a weakened immune system makes honey bees more vulnerable to the negative effects of pesticides?

Two things were clear: (1) there was likely no one single cause behind CCD but rather a number of causes; and (2) there was no shortage of possible theories as to why honey bees were disappearing. For example, many reports of disappearing honey bees came from commercial beekeepers who rented out their hives to farmers. Perhaps honey bees were stressed out from being trucked across the country two to five times during a growing season. During their travels they would have to put up with confinement and temperature fluctuations, and this stress might weaken them to infection and disease.

Were honey bees stressed out once they arrived at the crops they had to pollinate? They might have faced over-crowding with too many hives in one place, leading to less food to go around and therefore poor nutrition. Or were they assigned to crops that had lower nutritional value in terms of the quality of nectar and/or pollen that they provided? Where there is a large area of only one type of crop available (such as almonds), which we call monocultures, this would not give honey bees the variety of nectar and pollen in their diets that they would normally get from foraging in more natural environments, where there is a variety of flower types. Would these factors lead to a compromised immune system, and therefore weaken their defenses against disease and infections, and eventual collapse of the colony?

At one point some people were even blaming radiation from cell phones for causing the disappearance of honey bees. There was a very small study that was done in India, in which researchers placed cell phones inside two honey bee hives. They claimed that compared to two other hives that did not have cell phones, the cell phone hives contained fewer honey bees, the queens laid fewer eggs, there were fewer bees leaving and returning to the hives, and there was much less stored pollen and nectar.

But reading the report, things don't add up. The study reported no massive disappearance of bees or abandoned honey stores. Both are key traits of CCD. The researchers studied only four colonies and didn't rule out any of the other possible causes of CCD. Most importantly, many of the colonies affected by CCD in the United States were nowhere near cell towers or cell phones. The evidence simply isn't there.

A TANGLED WEB OF SUSPECTS

A number of years and many research studies later, we still don't know the exact causes behind CCD. However, scientists have identified some likely suspects. Figure 5-1 shows one theory that involves a complex relationship between parasites, pesticides, and pathogens. The diagram looks

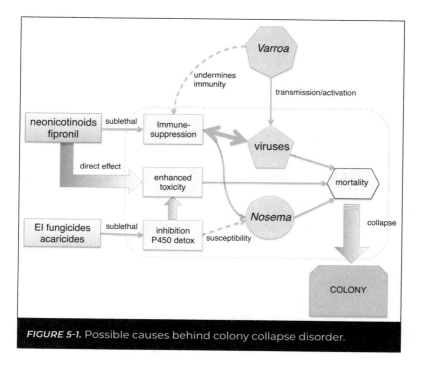

FIGURE 5-1. Possible causes behind colony collapse disorder.

pretty confusing, but if you walk your way through it, it makes more sense.

Starting at the top of the diagram, vampire mites are thought to contribute to the collapse of honey bee colonies in at least two ways. First, as they suck the blood out of a honey bee, they can transmit any of a number of different viruses to the bee. These viruses include acute bee paralysis virus, Israeli paralysis virus, Kashmir bee virus, and deformed wing virus. Vampire mites and all of these viruses are currently quite widespread across honey bee populations around the world, thanks to honey bee trading between countries and continents, and the transportation of hives for crop pollination. On their own, these viruses might cause no detectable symptoms in the bees. However, when combined with vampire mites, this might result in a deadly combination. There is evidence that when infected with vampire mites, a honey bee's immune system is greatly weakened, making it much harder for the body to fight off infection, such as a virus. With the honey bee's body unable to fight off the virus, the virus would have more of an impact— and in the case of most of the honey bee viruses mentioned earlier, this leads to spasms, paralysis, and eventually death.

Another way that honey bees' immune systems could be compromised, making them more vulnerable to viruses, is through the sublethal effects of pesticides. Two types of pesticides that affect honey bee health in particular are neonicotinoids and fipronil. Neonicotinoids, or neonics for short, are a group of pesticides that target an insect's brain and nervous system. If an insect eats enough of these pesticides, it causes paralysis and death. (There has been a lot of research on the effects of neonics on bumble bees, too. There will be a lot more to say about neonics and pesticides in general in the next chapter.) Fipronil also targets the insect brain and nervous system. Besides being used to treat crops, it is also found in a number of tick- and flea-control products for pets, as well as in some cockroach and ant traps. Scientists have shown that exposure to neonics or fipronil weakens a honey bee's immune system, making them unable to fight off the effects of any viruses they might be exposed to. The more their body is infected with one or more viruses, the sicker the bee becomes. Honey bees can also become sicker and sicker the more they are exposed to the pesticides, even without being infected by viruses. This way, as shown in Figure 5-1, the bees can die from the pesticides directly.

Figure 5-1 also shows that something called *Nosema* has been suspected as a cause of CCD. This refers to a single-celled parasite called *Nosema ceranae* that invades the honey bee's gut and gives it diarrhea. It also weakens the bee and makes it increasingly difficult for the bee's body to absorb any nutrients when the bee eats. Vampire mites, and/or exposure to pesticides, which weakens the honey bee immune system, can make honey bees more susceptible to the effects of the *Nosema* parasite. Sometimes honey bee colonies on the brink of collapse, or honey bees left behind from a hive afflicted with CCD, contain both *Nosema* and one or more viruses.

Finally, Figure 5-1 shows other culprits that are suspected causes of CCD: a specific type of fungicide called ergosterol inhibiting fungicides (EI fungicides) and acaricides. Acaricides are a group of chemicals used to treat ticks and mites. EI fungicides and acaricides seem to reduce the ability of the honey bee body to get rid of toxins (poisons), which is called lower detox. This somehow makes honey bees more vulnerable to the effects of *Nosema*, and since they alter the ability to cleanse the system of toxins, they can also make honey bees more vulnerable to the effects of pesticide exposure. What's really tricky is that many beekeepers treat their hives with a number of acaricides to prevent vampire mite infestation. When combined with the exposure to some pesticides, the acaricides become several times stronger, to the point that they become toxic to the honey bees.

It is very hard to get to the bottom of CCD because we still haven't found the bodies of the honey bees that have disappeared. Like any murder mystery, without bodies, there can be no autopsies. Also, out in the field, honey bees (and other species of bees) are exposed to a number of chemicals at once: field crops are often treated with a number of pesticides, herbicides, and fungicides. It is very difficult, if not impossible, to isolate the effects of each of them on bees, especially since the chemicals have been applied to crops in combinations for years.

WHAT ABOUT BUMBLE BEES?

So far CCD only seems to affect honey bees. There have been no mysterious mass disappearances of bumble bees from commercial colonies. When it comes to wild bumble bee colonies, however, we cannot be 100 percent confident that they haven't been disappearing, too. Wild bumble bee nests are very tricky to find, so it is hard to keep track of the health of wild populations. If wild bumble bees have been abandoning their nests and disappearing, we simply wouldn't know. Unless, of course, we come across a number of empty bumble bee nests. That hasn't happened—yet.

One of the main suspects behind CCD, vampire mites, so far only targets honey bees. It is a mystery why these mites target honey bees and not bumble bees. For some reason, they do not latch onto bumble bees and suck out their blood. However, looking at Figure 5-1, viruses and pesticides might also be behind CCD, and bumble bees have certainly been exposed to these. Perhaps bumble bees have been exposed to the same factors that lead to CCD in honey bees, but bumble bees react differently? Perhaps they don't abandon their nests, but behave differently, or just die? Or maybe

CCD truly is only affecting honey bees.

CCD does have an impact on the commercial production of bumble bee colonies, though, because in order to raise bumble bee colonies, you need pollen. Loads of pollen. Let's say a company raises one million bumble bee colonies each year. They would need around five hundred metric tons of pollen on an annual basis. That's equal to the weight of about eighty-five elephants! And that's just a conservative estimate. Across the world, each year, way more than one million colonies are shipped to farmers. That's a whole lot of pollen. The only way commercial bumble bee companies can get so much pollen is from honey bees. If beekeepers lose their honey bees to CCD, there will be no supply of pollen to the bumble bee companies. This would leave farmers of greenhouse tomatoes and other fruits and vegetables without bumble bees to pollinate their crops.

If there was any good that came from CCD, it's that the plight of bees was thrust into the public spotlight. The media went wild over the concept of "disappearing honey bees." There was a worldwide explosion of stories in newspapers, magazines, and on the internet. Public awareness of bees and their importance to our environment and food industry spread quickly. Unfortunately the focus has been on honey bees, and honey bees are generally what still comes to mind when people think of bees. The thousands of other bee species (including bumble bees) have not received anywhere near as much attention. But while public awareness of bees might be very narrow, at least bees, and the plight of bees, are on people's radar. Which is a good thing, considering there is one human-made threat that can cut across all bee species: pesticides.

CHAPTER SIX

Poisoning Bumble Bees

Farmers have a tough job. On top of all of the physical work they must do on a daily basis, they have to deal with dozens upon dozens of little critters that can eat their crops. There is a huge industry devoted to figuring out how we can manage these pests. Large companies have come up with chemical sprays, soil treatments, and other methods of treating crops so that they don't get eaten or otherwise damaged before they reach our plates. It is a constant battle, since insects can sometimes become resistant to these treatments over time, eventually making them useless. Or, there might be a new bug on the block that scientists have to figure out how to repel or kill.

In the early 1990s, one company, Bayer Crop Science, hit the jackpot when they discovered a new group of insecticides[1] in neonics (remember them from the last chapter?). These insecticides got their name from the fact that they have a similar chemical structure to nicotine, the addictive drug found in tobacco. Neonics attach to specific parts in the insect's brain and cause the insect to become paralyzed. Eventually, the insect dies.

This pest control method has several things going for it that made the folks at Bayer excited. For one, neonics only appear to affect insects. The pesticides seemed completely safe as far as humans and other animals go. And neonics turn out to be systemic pesticides. That means that the chemical is taken up by the roots of a plant, enters the sap, and travels to the plant's stem, leaves, flowers, and pollen. No matter which part of the plant an insect feeds from, it will end up eating the pesticide. All parts of the plant are completely protected.

Neonics can also be applied to crops using several different methods: as sprays, as granules scattered in the soil, or most commonly, as seed coatings. Seed coatings are thought to be a better method of applying pesticides to crops because with sprays, the chemical can drift with the wind and/or leach into soil and bodies of water. With seed coatings, the idea is the pesticide stays within the targeted plant.

---

1. *Insecticides* are anything that is designed to kill insects. *Pesticides* are anything that is designed to kill pests, which can include insects. So, insecticides can be considered types of pesticides.

But there are other uses for neonics besides protecting crops. They can be used to treat gardens, lawns, golf courses, and they can kill ants and termites. Some neonics are used as flea control for dogs and cats.

The first neonic that was approved for use as a pesticide was *imidacloprid* (we'll call it IM for short) in 1991. IM is sold under the names Confidor and Admire for sprays, and Gaucho for seed coatings. By 2009, IM was the largest selling insecticide in the world, valued at approximately $1 billion. By 2011, IM was registered for use for over 140 different crops in more than 120 countries.

A SILENT KILLER?

But while companies and farmers were celebrating the success of these pesticides, alarm bells started ringing elsewhere. In 1994, Gaucho entered the market in France as a seed coating for sunflowers. From 1995 onward, French beekeepers saw thousands of dead honey bees in front of their hives, and many of the remaining honey bees were acting strangely: They trembled, their tongues kept sticking out, and they kept grooming their head and antennae. There was also a very sharp decline in honey production. The problem seemed to get worse the more Gaucho was used, not only for sunflowers but also for corn. The beekeepers strongly suspected that IM was to blame for the honey bee deaths.

It turns out that IM, and in fact all neonics, are highly

toxic to honey bees. These chemicals make their way into the pollen and nectar of treated plants, which is then eaten by honey bees and other pollinators. Of course, neonics were not meant to target helpful insects, but the chemicals cannot tell the difference between the brains of a pest and the brains of a pollinator.

Evidence that honey bees were in fact eating neonics was provided by a study based in Switzerland, where scientists analyzed 198 honey samples from around the world.[2] The study was actually a citizen science project, led by the botanical garden of Neuchâtel, where people were asked to bring back local honey from wherever they traveled.[3] Over a hundred people provided over three hundred honey samples. The research team wanted a relatively balanced geographical coverage, but most of the samples were from Europe. So, to make sure Europe wasn't overrepresented, they narrowed down the number of honey samples to 198. In the end, honey from North America, Europe, Africa, South America, Asia, Australia, and New Zealand was analyzed. All continents were covered, including a number of isolated islands. (Well, all continents except for Antarctica. But there are no bees there.)

---

2. Since honey bees spit up nectar into a wax cell and then convert it into honey, the content of honey is a good indicator of what honey bees are eating.

3. *Citizen science* is a term for a project where non-scientist members of the public give their observations to the lead scientist(s). Their data may be used in the project.

When analyzing the honey samples, the scientists looked for traces of five commonly used neonics: acetamiprid, clothianidin, IM, thiacloprid, and thiamethoxam. Overall, they found some in 75 percent of all the honey samples. Eighty-six percent of the North American samples had neonics, and neonics were found in 80 percent of the samples from Asia, 79 percent of the samples from Europe, and 57 percent of the samples from South America. Thirty percent of all honey samples were contaminated with one type of neonic, 45 percent were contaminated with between two and five, and 10 percent had four or five. The conclusion was clear: Honey bees around the globe were eating nectar laced with chemicals.

It is important to point out that even though neonics have been deemed safe for humans, there are still regulations as to the maximum levels of the pesticides that can be found in our food. In the honey-from-around-the-world study, none of the honey samples that tested positive for neonics were above the limits set by the US and Europe. So as far as we know, none of the honey was hazardous to our health. It was a completely different story for honey bees, though. The levels of neonics found in the honey were high enough to cause problems with honey bee learning and behavior, a weakening of their immune system, growth disorders, lower queen survival, and it lessened their ability to collect pollen and nectar. So, if honey bees were not being killed by the pesticides, they were being exposed to sublethal effects.

As for Gaucho, the commercial seed coating for sunflowers that was blamed by French beekeepers for honey bee deaths, its use has been suspended in France since 1999. The United States, Canada, and the European Union now require by law that, for any pesticide, toxicity tests be carried out for honey bees. Specifically, what needs to be determined is called the LD_{50}: the dose of the pesticide that can kill 50 percent of a sample of honey bees. (LD stands for *lethal dose*.) The idea is that once we know this dose, crops will be treated with the pesticide at levels below that so honey bee deaths can be kept at a minimum.

This requirement to figure out the LD_{50} of pesticides for honey bees is well-intentioned, but there are still problems with this system. The pesticide companies aren't required to test which doses of the pesticide can cause harmful, sublethal effects in honey bees. They only need to figure out how much of the pesticide can *kill* half of a sample of honey bees. The LD_{50} doesn't test for a situation where honey bees could be exposed to doses of the pesticide over a long period of time. The dose amount in LD_{50} only measures the deadliness one dose of a pesticide or a series of doses over a very short period of time, such as within a day. And can we guarantee that pesticides will always be applied using the LD_{50} as a guide? Accidents do happen. Not to mention, the toxicity tests required by law are only for honey bees. What about effects on other beneficial insects, such as bumble bees? Can we assume that the levels of pesticide that can kill a honey bee are the same for other (very different) species of pollinators?

BEYOND HONEY BEES

Now consider this: Honey bees are not the only helpful insects being exposed to neonics. Despite how targeted they are meant to be, an average of 5 percent of the neonic coating on treated seeds is absorbed by the plant, meaning 95 percent of the chemical seeps into soil and water. That's a whole lot of neonics that are being spread into the environment with each crop treatment! And neonics have been found in wildflowers that grow beside fields of crops treated with the pesticides. That means the pesticide has seeped away from the area where they were applied (through the flow of soil water) and been taken up by other plants. What's more, repeated use of neonics on crops for more than one growing season increases the concentrations of those chemicals in soil and water. And neonics tend to stick around: They have been found in soil and water several years after application to crops had stopped. That means that they can persist in surrounding plants for some time.

So, wild pollinators, such as bumble bees, could

potentially be exposed to neonics if they gather pollen and nectar from flowering crops treated with the pesticides, and also if they forage from wildflowers surrounding the crop areas. Is there any evidence that bumble bees are in fact picking up harmful chemicals when they collect food from treated crops and surrounding wildflowers?

A research group in the United Kingdom ran a study to answer that question. They obtained eight commercial buff-tailed bumble bee colonies and placed five of them in different farmland sites in southeast England. The sites were at least 0.62 miles apart and were on average 0.37 miles from the nearest canola crop. (Canola blooms into bright yellow flowers that provide nectar and pollen. We use the oil from canola for cooking and baking at home, and restaurants use it, too.) So, at each site, the bumble bee colonies had the choice of collecting pollen and nectar from the canola crops and/or from the wildflowers that grew in the margins. The researchers confirmed with the farmers who owned the crops that the canola had grown from seed coatings treated with neonics.

For comparison, the remaining three commercial bumble bee colonies that were included in the study were placed in city gardens. These gardens were more than 2.49 miles apart and were on average 0.98 miles from the nearest canola field. Bumble bees tend to forage pretty close to their nest, so it was expected that the bumble bees from the three colonies would forage from flowers in the gardens rather than fly all the way to the canola fields. Unfortunately, the researchers weren't able to figure out whether or not these gardens had been previously treated with pesticides.

The researchers opened the entrances of all eight colonies and allowed the bumble bees to forage freely for four weeks during the blooming period of the canola crops. After those four weeks the researchers sampled the pollen that was collected and stored by each of the eight colonies. They identified which plant(s) the pollen came from and analyzed it for twenty different types of pesticides (neonics with some popular fungicides thrown in).[4] They also plucked three to eight worker bumble bees from each colony to test for the presence of pesticides in their bodies.[5]

Among the five colonies that had been placed in rural farmland, on average 32 percent of their pollen had been collected from canola flowers, and the rest of the pollen was a mixture from different wildflowers. So even though the bumble bee colonies were placed at a bit of a distance from canola crops, they nevertheless gathered quite a bit of pollen from them. Each pollen sample that was taken from the five

---

4. *Fungicides* are anything that is used to kill a fungus or fungi. They can be chemicals or little living creatures.

5. In order to be analyzed for pesticides, the poor bumble bees were frozen and ground up with a mortar and pestle. Not a happy fate for the bees, but at least they were contributing to science and the greater good!

nests contained between three and ten different pesticides: several different neonics along with a number of fungicides. Analyses of the bumble bee bodies also showed several different neonics and fungicides. The amount of pesticides in the pollen and bee bodies varied quite widely between the different colonies: Some colonies had very high concentrations of pesticides in their pollen and bees, whereas others had lower amounts.

What about the bumble bee colonies that were placed near city gardens? Five different pesticides were detected in their pollen samples, and three different pesticides were found in bumble bees. Compared to the bumble bee colonies that had been placed in farmland, the amount of pesticides in the pollen and bees were much lower. Still, it was clear that even in city areas far from commercial farms, bumble bees were being exposed to pesticides.

There are a lot of alarming things about this study. Regardless of whether bumble bees were in the countryside or in the city, they ate a cocktail of different neonics and fungicides. Some colonies had very high concentrations of the pesticides in their pollen, which is concerning, considering pollen is fed to developing bumble bee larvae.

Also, pesticides were found in the wildflower pollen, which means that the pesticides seeped from the treated canola crops into surrounding areas. Even though the researchers didn't test the stored nectar in the colonies, undoubtedly it contained a mixture of pesticides, too. And the researchers only screened pollen and bee bodies for twenty specific pesticides and fungicides. There are many more pesticides in existence. Farmers told the researchers that their fields had also been treated with a class of pesticides called pyrethroids. Unfortunately, the researchers did not screen the pollen and bee bodies for these chemical compounds because that required a whole different method (and the researchers could only do so much!).

If only we could say that because this field study was done in the UK, these results don't necessarily apply to other parts of the world. Alas, similar studies have been done in other countries, and their results don't paint a very happy picture for bumble bees, either. For instance, one field study in the south of Sweden placed bumble bee colonies near sixteen canola fields: Eight of the fields were treated with neonics, while the other eight were not. As expected, neonics were detected in the pollen and nectar stored in the nests of bumble bees placed near neonic-treated fields. Compared to the bumble bee colonies that were placed by fields that had *not* been treated with neonics, bumble bee colonies that were near neonic-treated fields did not grow as large and produced fewer males and new queens at the end of the colony cycle. Fewer males and queens ultimately mean a much smaller wild bumble bee population.

What is particularly interesting about this Swedish

study is that honey bee colonies were also exposed to all of the canola fields, and those colonies seemed unaffected. Bumble bees, but not honey bees, were being negatively impacted by the pesticides. Remember the toxicity tests pesticide companies are required to run. Can we really use the results of honey bee tests to determine the "safe" dose of neonics for other types of bees?

In another large study, bumble bee colonies were placed at thirty-three canola fields across Germany, Hungary, and the UK. Like the Swedish study, some fields were treated with neonics whereas others were not. Again, neonics seemed to cause fewer queens and male bees to hatch. There were differences found between the three countries, however, suggesting that something else was at play that was not captured by the study. Most surprisingly, traces of the neonic IM was found in the pollen and nectar stored in the colonies, and IM was *not* one of the neonics that had been applied to the crops! The bumble bees must have been foraging from plants that had been previously contaminated with the pesticide.

Over in North America, a group of Canadian scientists used nets to collect wild worker bumble bees that were foraging at twelve blueberry farms in the Fraser Valley in the province of British Columbia. Six of the farms had sprayed the blueberry plants with neonic pesticides (they called these farms the "conventional" sites), and six of the farms were organic, meaning they did not use pesticides. The scientists collected three different species of wild bumble bees, which also happened to be the most abundant species in that area: the fuzzy-horned bumble bee (*Bombus mixtus*), the yellow-fronted or yellow head bumble bee (*Bombus flavifrons*), and the black tail or black-tailed bumble bee (*Bombus melanopygus*). After the bumble bees were caught at the farms they were placed in individual vials and frozen. Once the bumble bees were brought to the lab, any pollen that was on their back legs was removed for analysis.

The scientists tested for traces of eighteen different pesticides in the bumble bee bodies and in the pollen the bees had collected. The only pesticide they found in the bumble bee bodies was diazinon, a pesticide that had been phased out of Canada about three years earlier from use in airblast sprayers like the ones used to treat blueberry fields. Both diazinon and IM were found in the pollen samples, including the pollen samples from bumble bees collected from the organic farms! The scientists suspected, however, that the diazinon was coming from nearby raspberry fields, as diazinon was not phased out from use on raspberry crops until a year after their study. It is also possible that the IM in the bumble bees' pollen was coming from other types of crops surrounding the organic blueberry fields.

But the bottom line? In this study, regardless of whether bumble bees were caught at conventionally sprayed or organic fields, they were being exposed to pesticides. Organic, pesticide-free blueberry pollen and nectar was available, but bumble bees were getting at least some of their food from somewhere else, and this food was contaminated with neonics.[6]

The biggest study to date on pesticide residues in bee colonies was conducted with honey bees. Even though the study did not include bumble bees, it is worth mentioning mainly because of its massive scale. The study involved honey bee hives from across twenty-three American states and one Canadian province. The research team tested for two hundred different chemicals (including neonics) in the wax found in nests, pollen stored in nests, and adult honey bees. The results were incredible. In the 259 wax samples, 87 pesticides were found, and an average of 8 pesticides were found in each sample. The highest number of pesticides found in a single sample was 39. In the 350 pollen samples, 98 pesticides were identified, with an average of 7 pesticides in each sample. The most pesticides in any one sample was 31. In 140 honey bee bodies, an average of 2.5 pesticide residues were found in each bee, with 25 being the highest number of pesticides detected in any one bee. Out

6.   This study done in the Fraser Valley also looked at the pesticide concentrations in hummingbird body fluid and fecal pellets (poop). Hummingbirds are another important pollinator. Not surprisingly, traces of neonics were found in the birds that were sampled.

of all the hundreds of samples, only one wax sample, three pollen samples, and twelve honey bee samples had no traces of pesticides.

Clearly, honey bees across the United States were being exposed to many pesticides across enormous areas. Who knows what kind of effects all these different mixtures of chemicals were having on their behavior and health? And chances are, if honey bees across the United States are consuming pesticides to such a large degree, wild bumble bees and other pollinators are being affected by pesticides, too.[7]

WHAT DO PESTICIDES DO TO BUMBLE BEES?

EFFECTS ON FOOD-GATHERERS

All of this research from the UK, Sweden, Germany, Hungary, Canada, and the United States paints a pretty convincing picture: Bumble bees are eating the pesticides that we apply to our flowering food crops. The next question is, does this have any effect on bumble bee behavior and health? We saw that in some of the studies, there were smaller colony sizes and fewer new queens and males produced by bumble bee colonies placed next to neonic-treated crop fields. Do pesticides cause any other sublethal effects in bumble bees?

---

7. Studies like these are important to help us figure out what kind of impact our farming is having on bees. Unfortunately, they don't come cheap. In this big study, just to analyze the samples for the different pesticides cost nearly $175,000!

A number of scientists have tackled this question. Some fed bumble bees nectar and/or pollen that is treated with pesticides, and then watched for any effects on the bumble bees' behavior. They usually do this in laboratory settings so they can control precisely how much pesticide the bees are exposed to, and to make sure the bumble bees' behavior cannot be explained by some other factor in the wild, such as bad weather or disease.

The different ways that scientists set up their experiments are quite clever. One research team in the UK kept buff-tailed bumble bee colonies inside their lab but hooked up each colony to a tube that led to a hole in one of the lab windows. That way, bumble bees could travel from their colony, through the tube, and then outside to collect pollen and nectar. The lab was at the Royal Holloway University of London in Egham, Surrey, where there were tons of surrounding wildflowers and gardens. So, when the bumble bees flew out of the lab, they encountered a colossal floral feast!

To keep track of which bumble bees left their colony and came back again, and also to keep track of when and how long the bees were gone, the scientists glued a small radio-frequency identification tag (RFID tag) to the thorax of each bumble bee. These tags looked like tiny computer chips. They weighed hardly anything at all, so they didn't affect the bumble bees' movement or flight. Attached to the tube that connected the bumble bee nest box to the lab window were RFID tag readers. When a bumble bee with an RFID tag ran past the readers, it was like scanning an item at the grocery store: The unique number from the bumble bee's tag was recorded by a computer. The computer recorded the time when the bee ran past and also when it returned.

So, once the research team had set up their bumble-bee-tracking system, what did they do? These scientists were curious about the possible effects of neonics and pyrethroid pesticides. They took forty commercial bumble bee colonies and split them into four groups of ten colonies each. The first group, called the control group, was given a supply of plain sugar-and-water mixture to eat as a substitute for flower nectar. The second group was the neonic group: The scientists put neonics into the sugar water at levels that the bumble bees would likely experience in the field. The third group was the pyrethroid group (we'll call it the P group for short). For this group, the scientists sprayed filter paper with the pesticide (again, at an amount that the bees would likely find outdoors) and placed the filter paper around where the bumble bees accessed their container of sugar water. That way, just like how the bumble bees would have to crawl and step on pesticide-sprayed leaves outdoors to get at the flowers they want to collect nectar from, the bumble bees had to walk across a pesticide-laced surface to get at their sugar water supply. Finally, the last group was called the mixture group, where each colony had both neonic-laced sugar water *and* a pesticide-sprayed surface that they had to cross to get at the sugar water supply.

The main idea behind this experiment was that none of the four groups were given any pollen. To get pollen, the bumble bees had to leave their nest, scurry up the tube leading to the laboratory window, and fly outside to find flowers. The scientists wanted to see if there were differences in the pollen collection of the bumble bee colonies in the three groups that were exposed to pesticides versus the colonies in the control group. Any effect on pollen collection could have serious consequences for the survival of the whole colony. Developing larvae need pollen in order to grow into adult bumble bees, which become males and new queens that eventually establish new colonies.

To lower the chance that the bumble bee colonies in their lab were being exposed to pesticides from flowers outside, the scientists ran their experiment from July onward. People don't usually apply pesticides to flowering crops at that time of year. Also, to see if pesticide exposure affects colony development, at the beginning of the experiment all bumble bee colonies were very young: They all had at most ten worker bees when the scientists received them from the commercial company.

The scientists exposed the bumble bee colonies in the

neonic, P, and mixture groups to the pesticides for four weeks. At the end of this time a clear pattern emerged from the groups exposed to neonics. Compared to the colonies in the control group that were not exposed to any pesticides, the colonies that were given neonics actually had more worker bumble bees that went out to forage for pollen. However, the ability of these worker bees to bring back pollen was terrible! Neonic-exposed bumble bees brought back pollen loads that were much smaller, and on top of that, it took them longer to gather it. This would have serious effects on the overall colony. Fewer worker bees are in the nest to look after "housekeeping" duties, such as feeding larvae, regulating the temperature of the nest, and keeping the nest clean. There would also be much less pollen to feed developing larvae, which, as we learned earlier, ultimately leads to fewer males and new queens that can start new colonies.

But bumble bees with rotten pollen-collecting ability was not the only effect of neonics. Compared to control colonies, colonies that were given neonics had many more foragers that left the nest, flew outside, and became "lost." These bees simply never returned. By the end of the experiment, the neonic colonies produced much fewer larvae and pupae and had four times as many worker bumble bees die. Two of the colonies from the mixture group simply did not survive: One colony was dead three days into the experiment, and the other was dead eight days in.

These results were a horrible sign. Bumble bees in the experiment were exposed to levels of pesticides that wild bumble bees would encounter in the fields. Sure, the pesticides had been approved for use, because they didn't kill a particular number of honey bees. But the experiment shows that use of these pesticides, even within approved levels, can inflict disastrous effects on bumble bees.

Another experiment confirmed that bumble bees are not very good at gathering food when exposed to neonics. Bumble bees were given a low dose of neonics and then allowed to gather nectar from three different colors of artificial flowers. Compared to bumble bees that were not exposed to neonics, the exposed bumble bees were slower to start foraging, visited fewer flowers, and did not visit all three flower colors as often. This was not a result of their flying abilities being affected: The neonic-exposed bees flew just as fast as the bumble bees that were not exposed to the pesticide. So, on the surface the bumble bees might have seemed healthy—flying around like "normal" bees—but a closer look revealed that neonics were affecting them in more subtle ways. They may actually lower a bumble bee's motivation to forage. Lower motivation to forage can result in less food for colonies, making bees more susceptible to malnutrition, illness, and disease, and ultimately lead to a suffering bumble bee population.

EFFECTS ON "HOUSEKEEPING" BEES

Worker bumble bees that stay in the nest are also exposed to pesticides, because they drink the nectar that the foragers collect from outside. Do pesticides affect the behavior of the "housekeeping" bumble bees?

One research group from the United States ran an experiment in which they tracked individual bumble bees in their nests. The scientists glued a tiny square of waterproof, tear-resistant paper onto the thorax of each worker bee from eighteen colonies of commercial common eastern bumble bees. Each little square of paper had a unique arrangement of pixels on it (see Figure 6-1). Video cameras recorded the activity inside of each bumble bee nest, and a computer program was able to track the behavior of each bumble bee using their individual tag (see Figure 6-2). The scientists called this system of tags and computer software BEEtag: **BE**havioral **E**cology tag.

FIGURE 6-1. Left: An example of a bumble bee with a BEEtag. Right: A close-up view of the unique arrangement of pixels on the BEEtag.

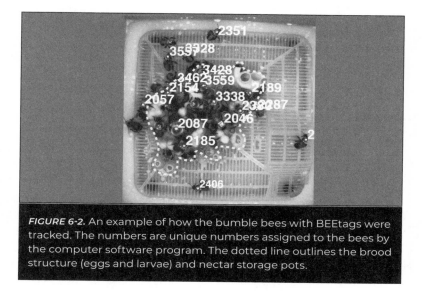

FIGURE 6-2. An example of how the bumble bees with BEEtags were tracked. The numbers are unique numbers assigned to the bees by the computer software program. The dotted line outlines the brood structure (eggs and larvae) and nectar storage pots.

In the experiment, nine colonies were given plain sugar water to eat (the control group), and nine colonies were given sugar water laced with similar levels of neonics that bumble bees would find when foraging from flowering crops. Compared to bumble bees in the control group, bumble bees that were exposed to neonics were less active, did not spend as much time looking after the larvae, and instead of clustering in the center of the nest where the brood and other worker bees are, tended to hang out alone around the outside edge of the nest. Even the queen bumble bees from the neonic-exposed colonies tended to be less active and not look after the larvae as much.

The second part of the experiment involved seeing whether exposure to neonics affects how well bumble bees in the nest keep the temperature warm and steady—an activity called *thermoregulation*. The scientists placed another eighteen commercial common eastern bumble bee colonies outdoors this time. But again, nine of the colonies received plain sugar water while the other nine had neonics in their sugar water. The scientists tracked both the outdoor temperature and the tem-

FIGURE 6-3. A photo of the inside of a healthy bumble bee nest showing a partially constructed wax canopy (black arrows and black dashed lines) covering the brood.

perature inside each of the colonies. They found that compared to the control colonies, the colonies that were exposed to neonics generally had a nest temperature that was colder, suggesting that they were not doing as good a job with thermoregulation. Also, to help keep the nest warm when it is cold outside, bumble bee workers usually build a wax canopy over the brood (see Figure 6-3). Eight of the nine control colonies built a canopy over their brood, but none of the nine exposed colonies did.

These experiments show us that pesticides can not only affect how bumble bees are getting their food, but how they perform their "housekeeping" duties as well. If pesticide exposure causes less pollen to be gathered by foragers and less care to be given to developing larvae, this can have very serious consequences for the health of bumble bee colonies, both present and future.

EFFECTS ON QUEEN BUMBLE BEES

Yet another way that pesticides could affect bumble bee colonies is through harming queen bumble bees. Queen bumble bees emerge from hibernation in spring, and they must forage on their own before they have established a nest full of worker bumble bees. It is during this vulnerable time when they are starting their own nest that they could be exposed to pesticides.

To find out whether pesticides can in fact affect queen bumble bees, another group of scientists in the United States purchased a number of queen bumble bees from a commercial company. The queens had mated and had just come out of hibernation, so they were ready to start their own nests. The scientists put each queen in her own little wooden nesting cage. Each cage had two sections. One section of the cage was dark to mimic a normal underground nesting situation, and it was in this section where the queen could start laying her eggs. The other section was exposed to light and contained a small container of sugar water, which would simulate aboveground foraging. Some queens received plain sugar water and a plain ball of pollen, and other queens received sugar water and pollen balls that had been treated with various levels of neonics. These queens were given the neonic treatment for eighteen days. This length of time, and the particular amounts of neonics that they were given, reflected a normal flower blooming period in the environment during which queens could be exposed to pesticides while they are foraging for pollen and nectar.

The results were quite concerning. Up to 65 percent of queen bumble bees that had been given neonics died, and it didn't matter whether the queens were exposed to a low level of the pesticide or a high level. For the neonic-exposed queens that survived, they started laying eggs much later than the queens who had been given plain sugar water and pollen. This delayed colony development could pose quite a problem, because when the adult worker bumble bees eventually do emerge, they would be out of sync with the blooming times of flowers in the environment, resulting in less available food for the colony.

Another study that exposed queen bumble bees to realistic levels of IM had similar results. Queens that ate IM-laced nectar long-term (thirty-seven days) were six times more likely to die compared to queens that were given plain nectar. The IM-exposed queens that survived were also less active and produced much less larvae and pupae compared to queens that were not exposed to IM. These studies strongly suggest that queen bumble bees are particularly vulnerable to sublethal levels of neonics that could be found in their environment when they are first trying to create a nest.

YUM, PESTICIDES!

Some people criticize laboratory studies that test the exposure of pesticides on bees. They claim that bees are forced to eat the pesticide-laced nectar or pollen during the experiments and are given no other food to choose from. They suggest that wild bees have the choice to avoid the pollen and nectar of pesticide-treated crops. However, these arguments assume that bees can detect pesticides in nectar and pollen. Can bumble bees tell when nectar or pollen is tainted with pesticides? And if they can, do they choose to avoid it?

A research group from the UK and Ireland designed an experiment where worker bumble bees were placed in their own individual plastic boxes for twenty-four hours and allowed to drink nectar from two different types of tubes. One tube provided the bees with sugar water, and the other tube provided sugar water that contained a particular concentration of neonics. The concentrations ranged from high to low and matched those that had been detected in actual food crops.

It turns out that when given this choice between plain sugar water and sugar water with pesticides, bumble bees preferred to drink the sugar water with pesticides! Interestingly, newly hatched worker bumble bees avoided the sugar water with pesticides and instead drank the plain sugar water; it was the older worker bumble bees that preferred the pesticides. Also, bumble bees that ate the pesticide-laced sugar water ate less overall compared to a group of bumble bees that were only given plain sugar water. Finally, the bumble bees chose to eat the pesticide-laced sugar water even though it lowered their chance for survival—a number of bumble bees ended up dying.

The fact that bumble bees chose to eat nectar that was laced with pesticides showed that they can detect pesticides somehow. So, the same research group measured the reactions of bumble bee nerve cells that detect different tastes. When they exposed these nerve cells to different concentrations of the neonics, the nerve cells didn't react. So bumble bees can't taste neonic pesticides in nectar. But then how are bumble bees able to tell the difference between plain nectar and nectar that has pesticides in it? The researchers think that the pesticides cause some kind of reaction in a bumble bee's brain, which somehow ultimately makes bumble bees choose to eat the pesticide. The degree to which bumble bees are conscious of this difference between plain nectar and pesticide-laced nectar is a whole other question entirely.

Another group of scientists, also from the UK, ran a similar experiment. They hooked up commercial bumble bee colonies to small flight arenas, and in the arenas, there were two types of feeders: one type offered plain sugar water, and the other type offered sugar water that was contaminated with neonics. For ten days the bumble bees were able to gather sugar water from whichever feeder they wanted. Again, bumble bees skipped the plain sugar water and opted for the sugar water laced with pesticide. Partway through the experiment the researchers changed the positions of the two types of feeders in the arenas. The result? The bumble bees found the new positions of the pesticide-containing feeders and continued to gather sugar water from them. Again, the bumble bees seemed to have a preference for pesticide-laced nectar, and they could somehow distinguish it from plain nectar.

If these experiments do in fact reflect what wild bumble bees are doing—choosing to gather nectar from contaminated flowers and crops—this means that they will bring pesticide-laced nectar back to their colony, exposing all of the bees in their nest to the chemicals, including new worker bees, queens, and males. Also, continuous gathering of pesticide-laced nectar leads to bumble bees being exposed to higher and higher levels of the pesticide, levels beyond what scientists may have previously predicted. And it shows that planting pesticide-free flowers for bumble bees might not be enough to prevent them from being exposed to sublethal effects of harmful chemicals: The bumble bees could possibly choose pesticide-contaminated plants anyway.

CAN WE LIVE WITHOUT NEONIC PESTICIDES?

A ton of evidence shows that neonic pesticides are putting bumble bee health in danger. But the reason humans use these pesticides is to protect food crops so that ultimately we can put food on the table. If we stop using neonics, will crops be destroyed by insect pests? Would we have less food to eat?

These questions were actually put to the test in 2013. The European Union placed a two-year ban on three of the most widely used neonics. It was hoped that during this ban more research would be done to see just how much impact the pesticides were having on bees.

But during these two years without pesticides, did farming in Europe collapse? Some pesticide companies predicted it would. One report funded by two big pesticide companies, Bayer and Syngenta, stated that if a ban was put into effect, billions of dollars and thousands of farm jobs would be lost. The reality? A number of crops in Europe, particularly corn and canola, actually had a slight *increase* in production. The doomsday predictions of the pesticide companies simply did not come true.

Research from across the United States tells us that farming would continue just fine without neonics. Soybean, corn, sunflower, cotton, and peanut crops that are grown from seeds coated with neonics have been compared to crops that have been grown from untreated, normal seeds. Overall, the treated seeds have not produced more or better crops. In many cases, the untreated crops produced *more* food.

Many research studies in the United States have focused on corn. This is because neonic-coated corn seed is the most widespread use of an insecticide on any crop in the United States—almost ninety million acres of farmland! These studies have basically shown that coating corn seeds with neonics is unnecessary. Scientists found that most of the insect pests that neonics are supposed to protect the corn from simply do not exist in numbers that would have a major effect on corn crops. And when pests do exist, they can be treated by other, more environmentally friendly farming practices. Also, neonics in corn plants can actually kill insects that prey upon corn pests. But the kicker is that there is no evidence that neonic-treated corn seeds regularly produce better crops compared to corn crops grown from untreated seeds. In some cases, neonic-treated seeds have actually resulted in *less* food and *less* profit for farmers.

If research shows that treating food crop seeds with these pesticides is unnecessary—and in some cases, is even harmful—why do we still do it? One reason could be that it is difficult for farmers in the United States to buy seed that is *not* treated with chemicals. Some studies have shown that between 71 to 100 percent of corn seeds are coated with neonics! Another reason is that pesticides are "cheap insurance" for farmers: They protect crops against the *potential* threat of pest infestations, and they require very little, or no, effort. In the case of coated seeds, the farmer doesn't need to provide any extra labor because the seeds are already prepared by the pesticide companies. They are convenient: The farmer simply has to plant them.

But the effects of these pesticides on the environment are severe and disturbing. We saw the effects neonics can have on bumble bee health and survival. Remember we learned that only about 5 percent of the neonic treatment is absorbed by the targeted plant. The remaining 95 percent of the chemicals escape into the soil, water, and surrounding plant life. We have only begun to scratch the surface in terms of understanding the effects these pesticides are having on plants and animals in the environment.

On the bright side, in 2018, the three most widely used neonics were banned indefinitely for outdoor use in European Union countries. (The pesticides could still be used within enclosed greenhouses.) In 2018, Canada also proposed to phase out the same neonics within three to five years. This period of time would allow farmers and other agricultural producers to find new forms of pest control for their crops.

The proposed ban was actually motivated by findings that levels of neonics in water systems are so high that they pose a serious danger to aquatic invertebrates. This includes freshwater mussels and insects such as dragonflies and mayflies. They are food for larger animals such as fish and reptiles, they help control pests like mosquitos, and they help maintain good water quality in nature.

These recent bans on neonics are steps in the right direction. Surely there is a balance that can be reached between ensuring enough good food crops for humans and protecting the welfare of bumble bees and other animals with whom we share this planet. This balance will require more effort on our part, a willingness and commitment to do things differently, and decision-making that is based on scientific evidence. This will all take time and money. But if the alternative is the eventual disappearance of bumble bees—and likely other animals as well—isn't the investment worth it?

CHAPTER SEVEN

Bumble Bee "Smarts"

When I was a student working in a bumble bee laboratory, one of the tasks I was often given was to "train" worker bumble bees to collect nectar (a sugar-and-water mixture) from fake flowers. At the time, the lab was in a room in the basement of a university building. The room was brightly lit, though—just like sunshine for the bees—so it didn't really feel like we were in a basement. Each box of bumble bees that we used, which was either bought from a commercial company or raised on our own from wild-caught queens, was connected to a large screened flight cage. The flight cage sort of looked like a gazebo. The worker bumble bees in the box had never flown outside and had never seen flowers. It was my job to introduce the bumble bees to the flight cage and the artificial flowers that we placed inside it before we could begin our experiments.

Each box of bumble bees was connected to the flight cage by a little wooden, glass-covered hallway, so you could see which bumble bees were coming and going from the box. There were a couple of plastic "gates" that we inserted in the glass hallway that I could lift up and down to control which bees entered the cage and which bees could return to their nest. When I was training the bees, I would just lift the gates out completely to let them come and go as they pleased.

It was funny because the "flowers" we placed in the cage for the bumble bees didn't look like flowers at all. They were little wooden boxes, each with a bright yellow removable plastic surface. There was a little hole in the plastic, just big enough for a bumble bee proboscis to slip through. When a bumble bee stuck its proboscis into the hole, it could drink a little bit of nectar. After a bumble bee drank from the flower, all I had to do was press a button on a keypad out-side of the cage, and the flower would refill for the next bee.

Each one of these flowers was stuck to a pole about waist high, and we could place the end of the pole in a hole in the floor of the flight cage. There were holes all over the floor of the flight cage, so we could pretty much stick the flowers anywhere inside it.

When I trained a new colony of bumble bees, I would set up some of the artificial flowers in the middle of the flight cage, remove the gates in the bee hallway, and sit back to watch.

At first there was always a mad rush: A whole bunch of bumble bees would scurry down the hallway and launch themselves into the flight cage. They would fly around and around, ignoring the flowers at first as they tried to get their bearings inside the cage. The buzzing of all of those wings created a loud hum in the room—a hum that was quite calming.

Many bumble bees would eventually find their way back to the nest and stay there. But several bees always found the flowers. After taking a drink they would fly straight back to the nest. A few moments later I would see these same bees leave the nest again. (I could tell the bees apart because I had glued little numbered tags to them.) The bees would scuttle down the hallway, in quite a hurry, and fly straight to the flowers. Back and forth between their nest and the flowers they would fly, over and over, bringing food to their family. There was something so peaceful about watching these bees work. It also gave me time to think.

There were two things I saw that made me wonder whether there were more to bumble bees than meets the eye. First, if there was a bumble bee on an artificial flower in the cage, sometimes other bumble bees would land on the same flower, even though there were other similar flowers around it with no bumble bees. Did that mean bumble bees can learn from other bumble bees?

Second, when it came time to run an experiment, I used

the plastic gates in the hallway to only allow the good foragers into the cage. Sometimes specific bumble bees, who I knew were good foragers, would seem "impatient" when I didn't let them into the flight cage right away. They would actually hop up and down beside the gate until I opened it to let them through! They would also try to squeeze under the gate to lift it up. Were these bees actually feeling an emotion like impatience? Frustration? Anger?

Unfortunately, I didn't have the chance to design and conduct studies that could help answer these questions. But other scientists have asked similar questions about bumble bees and have conducted some pretty ingenious experiments. What they discovered about bumble bees is quite remarkable.

SOCIAL LEARNING:
THE STRING-PULLING TASK

Since my time in the bumble bee lab, scientists have found that when bumble bees encounter flowers they don't recognize, they tend to visit them if they are already occupied by another bumble bee. But if bumble bees do recognize a certain type of flower and there is another bumble bee on it, they will tend to avoid it. If you think about it, this makes sense. Bumble bees that are on an unfamiliar type of flower can act as a signal to other bumble bees that the flower is a good source of food, and that it is worth visiting to try it out. On the other hand, if a bumble bee already knows that a particular type of flower provides nectar, it is best to avoid a blossom that has a bee on it because the flower will likely be empty by the time the bumble bee gets to it.

So, maybe what I noticed years ago in the bumble bee lab was in fact bumble bees learning from other bumble bees. And there have been even more experiments that provide evidence of this skill, which we call social learning, in bumble bees.

Scientists who study animal behavior sometimes give animals puzzles to solve that they wouldn't normally encounter in nature. This allows us to see how flexible their behavior and problem-solving abilities are. A team of scientists from the United Kingdom, China, and Norway gave buff-tailed bumble bees a task where they had to learn to pull a string to get a reward—something bees don't need to do in the wild! As you can see in Figure 7-1, at first the bees were presented with artificial blue flowers that contained sugar water. Once bumble bees learned to drink the sugar water from the artificial blue flowers, the scientists started to make things a little trickier.

The scientists first tested whether bumble bees could figure out the puzzle all on their own. They attached a string to the artificial flower, and then they slid the flower underneath a small, clear, plastic table. In order to get to the sugar water that was in the middle of the flower, the bees had to tug on the string to pull the flower out from under the table.

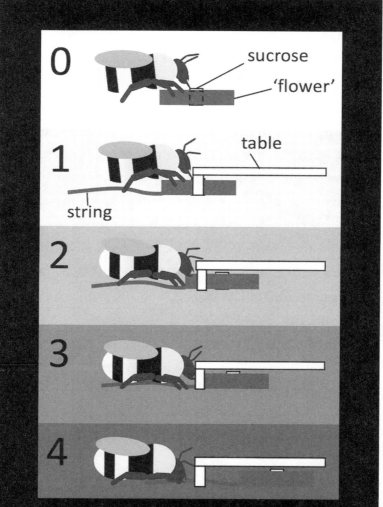

FIGURE 7-1. Steps used to teach bumble bees to pull a string to get a reward. Step 0: Bumble bees were given artificial blue flowers containing sugar water. Step 1: A string was attached to the flower, which was half covered by a transparent table. Step 2: Most of the flower was under the table. The bees needed to pull the string using either their legs or mandibles. Steps 3 and 4: The whole flower was under the table.

When the scientists set the bumble bees loose onto this scenario, did any of the bees solve the puzzle? Unfortunately, most did not. But they did seem to try their hardest to reach the flower through the top of the plastic table! Two superstar bumble bees managed to pull the string to reach the flower. These two bumble bees are described in the scientists' report as being "exceptionally explorative," meaning they tried a variety of ways to get at the flower under the table. Eventually, when reaching under the table, the bees accidentally moved the string, which in turn moved the flower, and the bees then figured out what to do.

Because the scientists tested dozens of bumble bees and only two solved the puzzle on their own, it is pretty safe to say that pulling a string does not come naturally to bumble bees. So, the rest of the bumble bees were trained to solve the string-pulling task, using the steps shown in Figure 7-1. In the end, out of forty bumble bees that underwent the

FIGURE 7-2. Photograph of a worker bumble bee, with an identity tag on its thorax, using its left front leg to pull a string attached to an artificial flower that is underneath a plastic table.

training, twenty-three of them learned how to solve the string-pulling puzzle. Not bad for a tricky task!

For their next experiment, the team of scientists wanted to see whether bumble bees could learn how to pull the string to get the sugar water simply by watching a trained bumble bee do it. After a new group of bees was allowed to learn to drink from the blue artificial flowers, they were each placed in a little, transparent, plastic chamber. They were then allowed to watch as a demonstrator bee solved the string-pulling puzzle ten times. Then the scientists gave the observer bees the chance to solve the string-pulling puzzle on their own. The result? Although they were a bit slow, over half of the observer bees correctly tugged the string to pull the flower out from under the table!

A last experiment tested whether this string-pulling behavior could spread through colonies. The scientists placed one bumble bee, who knew how to solve the string-pulling puzzle (the "demonstrator" bee), into a colony of bumble bees that had absolutely no experience with the string-pulling task. Then they allowed pairs of bumble bees into the arena that contained the string-pulling puzzle. The pairs were determined by the order in which the bees scurried down the hallway that connected the nest box to the arena; sometimes the pair included the demonstrator bee, and sometimes it didn't. The scientists found that after only 150 pairs of bumble bees had entered the arena and interacted with the string-pulling puzzle, a large number of bumble bees had learned how to pull the string to get the reward. The scientists did the same thing with two other bumble bee colonies and got the same results. The extra cool thing was that bumble bees who had learned how to pull the string from the demonstrator bee went on to "teach" other bumble bees how to do it. The new foraging skill had spread through the colonies.

Considering that in the wild bumble bees don't have to pull strings to get nectar from flowers, the fact that bumble bees could be taught to do so is pretty amazing. And the fact that demonstrator bees can help observer bees learn how to do it is extra impressive.

All of this was accomplished with brains that are about the size of a sesame seed. This means that some forms of complex problem-solving and the ability to learn from watching others don't require a brain that's as big as ours.

ON A ROLL: BALL-ROLLING BUMBLE BEES

Not only can bumble bees be trained to pull strings to get a reward, they can also be trained to roll a ball to a target. And they show some pretty impressive problem-solving skills in the process. Scientists from the United Kingdom used a small plastic model bumble bee attached to a thin transparent stick to demonstrate to worker bumble bees how to push a yellow ball into a circular target area on a platform. When the ball was rolled into this circle, the bumble bee would get a reward of sugar water to drink. Those bumble bees eventually learned how to roll the ball into the circle by themselves.

After the scientists trained a group of ball-rolling bumble bees, they ran an experiment under three conditions, as shown in Figure 7-3. Under the first condition, the ball-rolling bumble bees demonstrated the ball-rolling technique to bumble bees that were new to the setup. There were three balls, and the demonstrator bee always rolled the ball that was farthest from the center into the target circle. (The other two balls were glued to the platform and couldn't be moved.) There were three plastic guiding lanes on the platform to help the bees roll the ball toward the center (see Figure 7-3). The second condition was called the ghost condition. The scientists used a magnet under the platform to move the ball that was farthest from the target circle into the target circle. So the observer bees in this condition, who did not know how to roll a ball, saw the ball move, but it looked as though the ball was moving on its own. Bumble bees that were in the third condition saw no demonstration: The ball was already in the target circle with a drop of sugar water. Would observer bees from all three conditions learn to roll the ball that was farthest from the center into the target circle?

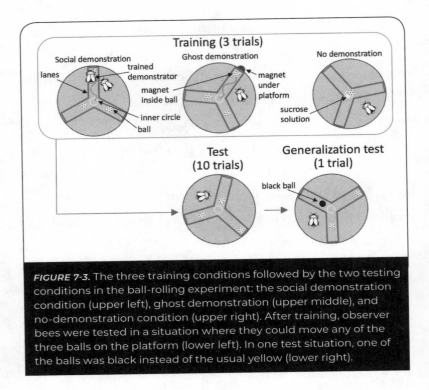

FIGURE 7-3. The three training conditions followed by the two testing conditions in the ball-rolling experiment: the social demonstration condition (upper left), ghost demonstration (upper middle), and no-demonstration condition (upper right). After training, observer bees were tested in a situation where they could move any of the three balls on the platform (lower left). In one test situation, one of the balls was black instead of the usual yellow (lower right).

The first thing the scientists observed was that observer bees who had had a live bumble bee demonstrator were more successful in rolling a ball to the circle target, and took less time to do so, compared to observer bees from the ghost condition and observer bees from the no-demonstration condition. However, observer bees from the ghost condition were better at rolling the ball to the target circle compared to observer bees from the no-demonstration condition. This suggests that just seeing the ball move was enough for the bees to learn to roll it on their own. Nevertheless, there was something about seeing an actual bumble bee rolling the ball that was most helpful for the observer bees to learn the task.

Now for the really cool part. Remember that during training, only the ball farthest from the center could be moved; the other two balls were glued down. When the observer bees were tested, however, no balls were glued, so they could move whichever ball they chose. Instead of moving the ball that was farthest from the center, like what was demonstrated to them during training, most observer bees moved the ball that was *closest* to the center. They figured out a much easier way to solve the problem! And not only that, but when the ball closest to the target was colored black, the observer bees still moved that ball into the circle.

What is so remarkable about these results is that not only did bumble bees learn how to solve a completely new problem by watching other bees, they didn't just copy the demonstrators. The observer bees didn't just learn the rule, "move the farthest yellow ball into the circle." They learned some kind of overall concept of moving a ball into the circle, because they used a ball that was in a different position and of a different color than what was demonstrated to them. This may mean that bumble bees are much more clever than what we might think.

The string-pulling and ball-rolling experiments suggest that bumble bees can learn from other bumble bees. But that leads us to more questions. To what degree do bumble bees recognize other bumble bees? Do they recognize bumble bees from their own colony? Or do all bumble bees look the same to one another? Do bumble bees recognize other bumble bees as bumble bees, or simply as interesting objects that they are attracted to?

Some scientists found that when given a choice of things to approach—in one particular experiment, flowers, black discs, and live bumble bees—bumble bees chose to approach the live bumble bees. This suggests that bumble bees have

an attraction to other beelike things. But what it is about other bumble bees that bumble bees are attracted to remains a mystery. Their shape? Their smell? Their size? Their colors? The way they move? Some or all of the above? Only more experiments will tell.

FIGURE 7-4. A bumble bee rolls a ball during the ball-rolling experiment.

BEE HAPPY! EMOTION IN BUMBLE BEES?

Now, think back to those "impatient" bumble bees I watched. If bumble bees can learn by watching other bumble bees, and if they can learn a concept such as "roll a ball into a circle," is it possible that other stuff is going on in their heads? What about emotions?

Scientists who study human behavior have shown that if you give people a sweet snack, it tends to put them in a good mood. Researchers in the United Kingdom decided to try this with bumble bees: If bees were given a small drop of really sweet sugar water, would they then behave in a way that suggests they are experiencing positive emotions?

The way the scientists tested this was quite clever. They hooked up a box containing a colony of buff-tailed bumble bees to a small arena. Inside the arena were colored squares, and underneath each square was a tube that the bees could crawl into and drink from. Bumble bees learned that if they drank from the tube that was under a blue square, they would get sugar water (that is, a reward). If they drank from a tube that was under a green square, they would get regular water (which bumble bees find unpleasant). So, the bumble bees learned to approach blue squares and avoid green squares. But then the scientists presented the bees with an uncertain situation: a square that was colored blue green. What should the bumble bees do? Approach or avoid it?

Half of the bumble bees, as they traveled down the hallway that led from their nest box to the arena, encountered a surprise: a small drop of sugar water that was sweeter than what they had been getting from the feeder in the arena. So, they got a "sweet snack" before seeing the blue-green square. The other half of the bumble bees received nothing. The result? Bumble bees that received the sweet snack took less time to approach the blue-green square and crawl into the tube underneath (expecting a reward) compared to the bumble bees that did not receive a sweet snack. The scientists ran other experiments to make sure the bees that received the sweet snack weren't just more excited or faster fliers. The results were the same. It seems as though if bumble bees get a sweet snack, they see an uncertain situation more positively or optimistically.

But what about sweet snacks improving our moods? Could this be the case for bumble bees as well? To test this, the same team of scientists trained bumble bees to drink sugar water from a feeder in a small arena (see Figure 7-5). After they drank from the feeder ten times, and when they appeared for their next foraging trip, each bumble bee was held temporarily in the hallway connecting the nest box to the arena. Half of the bumble bees were given a surprise drop of very sweet sugar water, while the other half received nothing. After a ten-second delay, the scientists simulated a predator attack:[1] The bumble bees were gently squished underneath a stamp-like device

---

1.   One predator that bumble bees can encounter in the wild are crab spiders. These critters sit on flowers and wait, usually quite camouflaged, and when a bumble bee lands on a flower, they pounce on them! Often the bees escape after a brief struggle, but sometimes the bees are not so lucky and become the spider's next meal.

that was softened with a sponge. They were held there for three seconds. Quite a stressful situation for a bee! Then the bees were released into the arena, and the scientists noted how long the bumble bees took to start drinking from the feeder.

The scientists expected that bumble bees that received a drop of really sweet sugar water before being squished with a sponge would "emotionally recover" from that stressful situation more quickly, and drink from the feeder in the arena sooner, compared to bumble bees that did not receive a sweet snack. This is indeed what the scientists found.

Can we conclude from these experiments that bumble bees have emotions? Do these results suggest that back in my bumble bee laboratory days, when I blocked bumble bee foragers from entering the flight cage and they were jumping up and down, they were experiencing frustration or anger?

A number of scientists

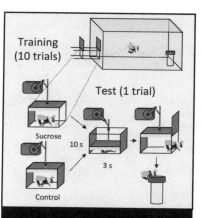

FIGURE 7-5. The top of the figure shows the arena where the bumble bees were trained to drink sugar water from a feeder. The rest of the figure shows some bees receiving extra-sweet sugar water while others received none, then being held for ten seconds, lightly squished, and released.

point out that we have to be careful when making guesses about behavior like that displayed by the bumble bees in these experiments. For one thing, emotions as we know them include a certain inner experience. We *feel* a certain way when we are happy; we *feel* another way when we are sad. In other words, there is a particular quality to an emotion that happens inside of us that we become aware of. This is called a subjective experience. The experiments that involved the surprise drop of extra-sweet water do not allow us to see the bumble bees' subjective experiences—or if they had any at all. We are unable to compare how the bumble bees *felt* compared to how we feel under particular circumstances. For this reason, some scientists argue that we cannot conclude that bumble bees have emotions. At least not yet, anyway. Perhaps if we can figure out a way to know exactly what bumble bees experience—peek into their inner world, so to speak—we can conclude whether or not what they are experiencing when encountering a surprise or a predator is, indeed, emotion.

Some scientists are also against jumping to the conclusion that bumble bees experience emotions because sometimes the behavior of nonhuman animals can be explained using much simpler terms. Perhaps the behavior of the bumble bees in the surprise sugar-water experiments doesn't need to be explained using a complex concept like "emotion." Perhaps the bumble bees who were given a sweet surprise flew to the blue-green square more quickly and recovered more quickly from being squished under a sponge not because the treat affected their emotions, but because it created in them a stronger motivation or drive to eat. Period. No emotions needed.

But why would a bumble bee that is trapped in a hallway and cannot fly to get food jump up and down? Maybe it simply had a very strong motivation or drive to collect food, but it also acted in a way that certainly looked like frustration! This is a good example of how easy it is for us humans to assume what someone (or some*thing*, like a bee) is experiencing, based on their behavior, which is how we might behave if we were in a similar situation. Projecting our emotions and subjective experiences to others like this comes naturally to us. It allows us to empathize, and to sympathize, with what others may be experiencing. It makes us want to comfort and help the individual, which ultimately supports the survival of our species.

Yet, until we can figure out the inner, subjective experience of a bumble bee, it is too much of a stretch to say they have a mental world that is anywhere similar to ours. That includes the experience of emotions—at least as we humans know them. But there is some recent research that suggests that bumble bees might have some form of a "mental life" after all.

SIGHTS AND SMELLS: DO BUMBLE BEES HAVE MENTAL PICTURES?

If you close your eyes, can you picture a circle? A square? How about a triangle? These shapes that you created in your head, and any other object that you might think about, are called mental representations. A really cool experiment suggests that bumble bees can create mental representations, too.

It all began with a very clever way to design artificial flowers. Scientists designed a white plastic disc "flower" that had twenty-four holes drilled into it (see Figure 7-6). In the middle of each flower the scientists placed a tiny plastic drinking cup. The scientists then covered the bottom of each disc with a sticky film, which transformed the holes into little wells that could hold a drop of liquid. They then placed eight drops of peppermint-scented oil into the wells of the discs; for five flowers the drops were placed in a circle pattern, and for five flowers the drops were placed in a cross pattern (see Figure 7-6). To make sure all the flowers looked the same, they filled the remaining sixteen holes in each flower with plain, unscented mineral oil. The only difference between the flowers was their scent pattern: a circle or a cross.

First, the scientists had to make sure that the bumble bees could tell the difference between the circle-scented flowers and the cross-scented flowers. So, they placed the

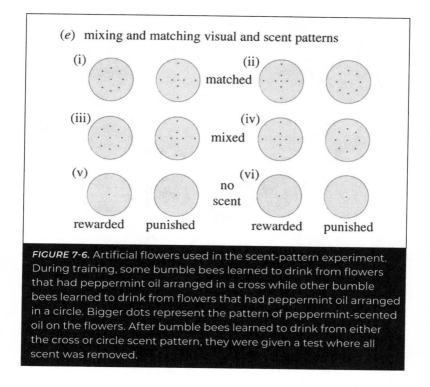

(e) mixing and matching visual and scent patterns

(i)   (ii) matched

(iii)   (iv) mixed

(v)   (vi) no scent

rewarded   punished   rewarded   punished

FIGURE 7-6. Artificial flowers used in the scent-pattern experiment. During training, some bumble bees learned to drink from flowers that had peppermint oil arranged in a cross while other bumble bees learned to drink from flowers that had peppermint oil arranged in a circle. Bigger dots represent the pattern of peppermint-scented oil on the flowers. After bumble bees learned to drink from either the cross or circle scent pattern, they were given a test where all scent was removed.

ten flowers in a small flight arena, each flower sitting on top of its own platform. They then connected a box of buff-tailed bumble bees to the arena. For half of the bumble bees that they tested, the circle-scented flowers had sugar water in their drinking cup and the cross-scented circles had plain water. The other half of the bumble bees had the reverse: the cross-scented flowers had sugar water while the circle-scented flowers had plain water.

Could the bumble bees tell the two scent-patterned flowers apart? You bet they could! When the circle-scented

FIGURE 7-7. A bumble bee on the surface of an artificial flower, where peppermint oil was placed in some of the holes.

flowers had the sugar water, bumble bees learned to drink from those flowers and avoid the cross-scented flowers. When the cross-scented flowers had the sugar water, bees drank from them and not the circle-scented ones.

Then came the incredible twist in the experiment. After the bumble bees learned which pattern had the sugar water, the scientists swapped out all of the artificial flowers with new flowers that only had a visual pattern on them. Five of the flowers had a circle pattern made out of red dots, and five had a cross pattern made out of red dots (see Figure 7-6). They had no scents at all. Then the bees were allowed to choose a flower. Remarkably, bees that had learned to visit circle-scented flowers landed on the flowers that had the red dots arranged in a circle, and bees that had learned to visit cross-scented flowers landed on the flowers that had the red dots arranged in a cross. Somehow the bees were able to match the scent patterns they learned with visual patterns they had never seen before! How did they do this? It could be that the bumble bees formed some kind of mental representation of the scent pattern they learned to visit—a circle or a cross. When they saw the visual patterns on the flowers, it was then a matter of matching them with the pattern they learned "in their head."

If this were the case, and the bumble bees formed mental representations of the shapes, can they form mental representations of anything else? Again, only more studies will tell.

AMAZING LITTLE BRAINS

Considering a bumble bee's brain is about the size of a sesame seed, it is quite amazing what they can accomplish. Not only can they find and remember the locations of flowers out in the big world, and do all the tasks necessary to keep their nest healthy, but the experiments described in this chapter show that bumble bees are able to adjust their behavior while foraging for food, depending on whether or not another bumble bee is present. It is also impressive that some bumble bees can be trained to solve problems by doing rather unnatural things, like pulling strings or rolling balls, and that some bees can learn from other bees how to do that. And bumble bees might experience something like emotions. On top of everything else, they seem to be able to form mental representations of scent-shapes. Incredible!

A bumble bee's brain contains about a million neurons (brain cells). Compare that to a human brain, which has eighty-five billion. Some scientists have been studying bumble bee brains to see what networks of neurons are involved when bumble bees learn and remember. Since bumble bee brains are much smaller than ours, it's easier to study them, and hopefully they can shed some light onto how human brains (and other animal brains) might be "wired," too.

Scientists have studied bumble bee brains and how they could work by creating networks of neurons using computer software. What they have mostly found so far is that the number of neurons that may be involved in, say, a bumble bee learning to approach one color and avoid another is much less than what might be expected. That is, in a number of cases, the computer software can simulate learning or a behavior using dozens or hundreds of neurons—not millions, as you may think. The connections between neurons also seem to be key: Each neuron can be quite complex, branching off in many directions, like an old maple tree. So, the ability of a bumble bee to learn something or perform a new behavior (like string pulling) might not depend so much on the *number* of neurons it has in its brain but the number and types of *connections* it can form between them.

So, if complex behavior like problem solving does not necessarily require lots of neurons, we might not marvel so much at how small bumble bee brains are but rather how well they are "programmed." But if bumble bees can do so much with so few brain cells, why do we as humans have so many? Maybe we should be marveling over how *big* our brains are!

Scientists are only starting to scratch the surface of how brains function, whether they are bumble bee brains or human brains. And based on the results of the experiments in this chapter, it is safe to say we are only starting to understand what bumble bees are capable of doing. What other mysteries are waiting to be unlocked in those efficient, impressive little brains of theirs?

CHAPTER EIGHT

Bumble Bees on the Brink

"The bee declines these days are a big concern. You know, it's like losing one of your relatives. To our people, it shows that we haven't respected them. We haven't done our duty or our obligations, our responsibilities. And so, the bees are leaving."

—Dr. Henry Lickers

THE MYSTERIOUS DISAPPEARANCE OF FRANKLIN'S BUMBLE BEE

Dr. Robbin Thorp knew the trails well in Mount Ashland, Oregon. He walked them regularly, with a butterfly net in one hand and a "bug vacuum" in the other. The bug vacuum looked like a big water gun. If Dr. Thorp pulled the trigger, it turned on a vacuum that sucked up whatever insect he was aiming for at the end of the tube. The bug was sucked into a transparent section where Dr. Thorp could see it more closely. After he identified the species, he set it free.

But Dr. Thorp wasn't looking for just any insect. He was searching for Franklin's bumble bee[1] (*Bombus franklini*; see Figure 8-1). It was now the year 2019, and the last time he spotted one was on August 9, 2006. He had frantically raced after it, but alas, it zipped away out of reach and disappeared across a field of yellow buckwheat. It was a thrill for him to see it, because at that point he hadn't seen any Franklin's bumble bees in three years. The species was becoming more and more rare.

FIGURE 8-1. Franklin's bumble bee, *Bombus franklini*.

Why was Dr. Thorp so interested in Franklin's bumble bee? The area in which this species lives is very small: from southern Oregon to northern California. That's it. Dr. Thorp wondered why Franklin's wasn't found in a wider area. And up until the 1990s, Franklin's was quite abundant in its region. Dr. Thorp saw many every day. Then something

---

1. Franklin's bumble bee was named in 1921 after Henry J. Franklin, who was the first person to describe the species.

happened after 1999. Suddenly, he didn't see any Franklin's anymore. Such a sudden loss in a species was unheard of. Why did it disappear? Dr. Thorp believed that finding some Franklin's bumble bees might help solve the puzzle.

Although he retired years ago after a long career as a professor, Dr. Thorp never stopped conducting his own surveys of Franklin's bumble bee. Each year, for eleven years, between 1998 and 2009, he searched from nine to seventeen sites where Franklin's bumble bees were found in the past, as well as six to nineteen additional sites where he hoped to spot the species. That's a lot of traveling, and a lot of searching.

After 2009, Dr. Thorp continued his surveys for Franklin's bumble bee, but he no longer prepared formal reports. The last time he saw a Franklin's, in 2006, it was a worker bee, which meant that somewhere out there was a nest. But if it was tricky to find individual bees, it was even harder to find where a colony was hidden!

Figure 8-2 shows the huge decline in the number of Dr. Thorp's sightings of Franklin's bumble bee. Although the graph ends at 2007, he kept looking for the bee up to 2019.

There are several strange facts surrounding the mysterious disappearance of Franklin's bumble bee. For one thing, there are still plenty of other species of bumble bees in the areas Dr. Thorp surveyed. Franklin's seems to be the only one missing. Why has Franklin's vanished while the other species are sticking around? Also, there has been little to no

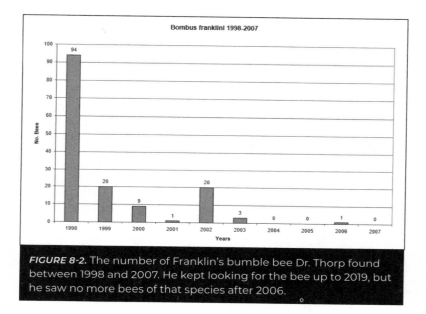

FIGURE 8-2. The number of Franklin's bumble bee Dr. Thorp found between 1998 and 2007. He kept looking for the bee up to 2019, but he saw no more bees of that species after 2006.

habitat loss:[2] Many of the sites where Franklin's used to be seen are parks, meadows, and trails that have been left relatively undisturbed over the years. There is still plenty of land where the bees can feed from flowers, find a nesting site, and hibernate for the winter. As far as we know, pesticides that are deadly to bees were not used in these areas.

Whatever it was that caused Franklin's bumble bee to vanish, it hit the species hard and it hit the species fast. There is one culprit that fits this description: disease. Dr. Thorp was the first to suggest that perhaps a pathogen

---

2.   *Habitat loss* is the shrinking in size of the natural area in which an animal lives, usually because of human activity.

that was not normally found in that area jumped from commercially raised bumble bees to wild populations. He specifically pointed the finger at *Nosema bombi*, or *N. bombi* for short, which is a fungus-type parasite. The reason? Around the same time that the population of Franklin's bumble bee crashed, commercial bumble bee companies reported massive outbreaks of *N. bombi* in their facilities. The outbreaks were so bad that they destroyed their stocks of the western bumble bee, to the point that they could no longer produce the species. Wild populations of the western bumble bee suffered, too. It made sense that if Franklin's bumble bee rapidly began to disappear at the same time, it was likely infected by *N. bombi* as well.

Dr. Thorp thought that the commercial bumble bees had introduced a new type of *N. bombi* to the wild populations to which the wild populations had no immunity. But with some scientific investigation, it was found that the type of *N. bombi* was not new at all. It was the same type that could be found in the wild. Commercial bumble bees, however, introduced more of it, likely when they escaped from greenhouses or when they were released into open fields to pollinate crops. And they introduced so much of it that the wild populations of the western bumble bee and Franklin's bumble bee couldn't cope, and as a result, they crashed. Other species of bumble bees, such as the ones that continue to be produced by commercial companies, and the ones that

Dr. Thorp continued to see during his surveys, somehow are not as affected by the fungus. At least, that's the theory. Unless we find more of Franklin's bumble bee, the cause or causes of its disappearance will remain a mystery.

Sadly, Dr. Thorp passed away on June 7, 2019. He was eighty-five and searched for Franklin's up until his last days. The world lost an authority and legend of entomology, the scientific study of insects. He never gave up hope for Franklin's bumble bee, and other scientists shouldn't either.

"STOP THE CAR!"

When Dr. Sheila Colla was a university student, she noticed something strange. She was out in the field helping another student collect bumble bees for his research on disease levels in wild bees. They were traveling throughout southern Ontario, in Canada. Dr. Colla had read a huge report put together in the 1970s that described a wide variety of bumble bee species that had been found in the region. But there was one species mentioned in the report that she didn't see: the rusty-patched bumble bee (*Bombus affinis*). It was as if this species had completely disappeared.

When she returned to the lab, Dr. Colla did some research and found that no one was really keeping track of bumble bee populations in Canada, or across much of North America. Was the rusty-patched bumble bee in fact starting to disappear? Was it in danger of dying off completely? Were there other species in the same boat? Or was she just unlucky and didn't see that species at the time?

Dr. Colla was hooked. She got to work.

First, she went back to the sites in southern Ontario and surveyed them more carefully. Between May and September 2004 to 2006, she went out with her field assistants, each carrying a butterfly net, and captured as many bumble bees they could find. When they caught a bumble bee, they identified the species, marked the bee with non-toxic bright-colored powder so they would know it was already counted, and then set it free.

After all of this fieldwork was finished, Dr. Colla and her colleague, Dr. Laurence Packer, compared the data to that of the big report that had been produced in the 1970s. They found that back in the '70s, the populations of the American bumble bee (*Bombus pensylvanicus*) and the yellow-banded bumble bee (*Bombus terricola*) were not very large, but those bumble bees were still quite present at those southern Ontario sites. In Dr. Colla's surveys, however, they found absolutely no individuals of those species. Even more disheartening was the state of the rusty-patched bumble bee: There had been many in the 1970s, yet Dr. Colla had found none of that species whatsoever. The evidence was clear: Over the past thirty-five years or so, those three bumble bee species had started to disappear.

Dr. Colla was especially worried about the rusty-patched

bumble bee. It had shown the most drastic loss of bees over the years. Also, the species is closely related to Franklin's bumble bee, which, she had learned from Dr. Robbin Thorp's work, was also in big trouble.

Thanks to that big report done in the 1970s, Dr. Colla knew that the rusty-patched bumble bee naturally lived in southern Ontario. Did it live anywhere else? If it did, and she went out and did more surveys, could she find it?

One way to figure out where a species can possibly be found is to use museum specimens or collections of bumble bees. These are bumble bees that were captured in the wild, killed, and then preserved (see Figures 8-3, 8-4, and 8-5). A bee specimen is stuck with a pin, which is then stuck through tiny pieces of paper on which the following information is written: the location where the bee was found, the date, what type of plant the bee was feeding on, the species of bee, the name of the person who identified it, and the date it was identified.[3,4]

Dr. Colla found a number of rusty-patched bumble bee

---

3. Bumble bee specimens also come in handy when scientists find bumble bees in the field that are tricky to identify. Some bumble bee species have very subtle traits that set them apart, and scientists can only confirm their identity by bringing the bee they caught back to the lab and then comparing it to another that they have on file.

4. It may seem cruel to kill bumble bees for study. However, bee specimens help scientists immensely when they are trying to identify species they caught in the wild, or when they are figuring out how widely a species is spread out over an area. Remember that a colony of bumble bees can have hundreds of worker bees, so losing one or two workers to science shouldn't impact a colony. Scientists do not kill queens of endangered species, since killing a queen prevents her from laying eggs to continue the species.

specimens from various museums and collections in Canada and the United States, some dating as far back as 1903. After noting the locations on the labels where all these rusty-patched individuals had been found, she had a pretty good idea of the range of this species. She then set off on road trips to see if she could still find them in those places. She visited forty-three sites in total: eighteen in eastern Canada and twenty-five in the eastern United States. After surveying all these sites, and catching and identifying about nine thousand bumble bees in total, she found only *one* rusty-patched bumble bee, foraging on a sunflower in Pinery Provincial Park in Ontario, Canada.

"The last rusty-patched bumble bee known from Canada," Dr. Colla said in 2019. "I was actually sitting in the passenger side of a car, looking out the window, and I saw it on the road. I told my friend to stop because I saw a bee that looked a bit different. And then we caught it. That was in 2009. And that's the last one that's been seen in Canada. No one has seen it since then."

What could be the cause of this drastic loss of the rusty-patched bees? Scientists such as Dr. Colla have suggested a number of possibilities: disease spreading from commercial bumble bee colonies (and/or perhaps from honey bee colonies) into wild bumble bee populations; pesticide use; land for nesting sites and flowers being taken over by large fields of food crops and/or the building of cities and roads; the

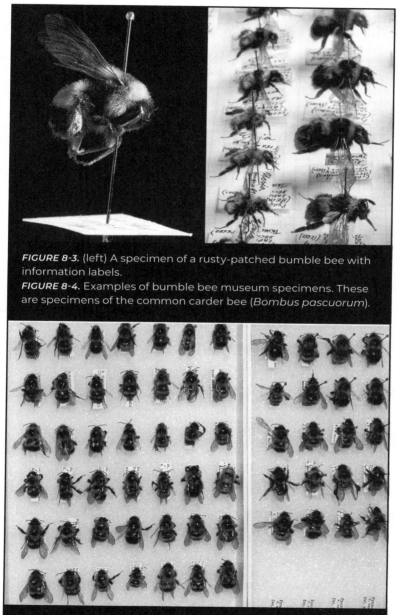

FIGURE 8-3. (left) A specimen of a rusty-patched bumble bee with information labels.
FIGURE 8-4. Examples of bumble bee museum specimens. These are specimens of the common carder bee (*Bombus pascuorum*).

FIGURE 8-5. An example of bumble bee specimens in a drawer where they are stored away from light damage and potential pests.

introduction of more honey bees, which creates competition for food; and climate change (for example, increased rain or drought). To complicate matters, there is likely not just one cause. Depending on where bumble bee colonies are located, they could be faced with two or more of these factors at once.

Dr. Colla also points out in her report on the rusty-patched bumble bee that bumble bees are much more vulnerable to extinction than many other animals. They need three different types of habitats, all located near one another: They need a place for a nest; a place to find flowers for nectar and pollen; and a spot where new queens, after they mate, can hibernate during the winter.

From what we know about their nesting behavior, bumble bees tend to choose underground nests that were once homes for mice, voles, or other rodents. If those animals are driven out of their habitat, this impacts the ability of bumble bees to find nests, too.

In terms of flowers for bumble bees, a good source of pollen and nectar needs to be located not too far from their nest. The rusty-patched bumble bee is a short-tongued species, which could limit the types of flowers it can visit. They would need flowers with short nectar tubes, otherwise they would not be able to reach the nectar. However, back when the rusty-patched bumble bee was more abundant, it was seen biting holes in the side of some flowers' nectar tubes and sucking out the nectar from there. Rusty-patched bumble bees need a varied, constant supply of flowers in their habitat. They need flowers that bloom from early spring, when the queens are establishing their nests, throughout spring and summer when the colony is growing, and into early fall when new males and queens need food until they mate.

In order for the queen bumble bees to hibernate safely over the winter, they need undisturbed soil where they can bury themselves underground. Digging up land, whether for crops or for building cities, houses, or roads, destroys the places where bumble bees hibernate, and disturbs or even kills the bees if they are already hibernating.

All of this suggests that the best habitat in which the rusty-patched bumble bee can thrive is undisturbed woodland, meadows, or perhaps large parks or gardens, with plenty of flowering plants that are native to the rusty-patched bumble bee's range. Undoubtedly this type of land would help other bumble bee species thrive, too.

Bumble bees are quite vulnerable to extinction because of their genetics and breeding behavior as well. If the population of rusty-patched bumble bees (or any other bumble bee species for that matter) becomes too small, then males start breeding with queens that are closely related to them, which is called inbreeding. This will cause new generations to have less genetic variety,[5] which can cause them to be less able to ward off stress and infections. Also, male bumble bees in the new generations might become sterile, meaning they cannot help to produce new bees. With new queens unable to create new colonies, bumble bees would disappear pretty fast. Inbreeding can happen if the population of a bumble bee species becomes fragmented. For example, if we build farmland or a city block or a road in the middle of a bumble bee habitat, these new structures separate and isolate bumble bee colonies that were once able to interact with one another. These new pockets of smaller bumble bee populations would not have as much genetic variety, and inbreeding can result.

Scientists have a pretty good idea what caused the population of rusty-patched bumble bees to be in danger: The spread of disease from commercial bumble bee colonies. Given how quickly the species disappeared, the timing of the decline in the population (specifically, after commercial colonies started to be used), and that commercial colonies often carry disease, it makes sense that a great number of the rusty-patched population probably became sick and died. This species is now listed internationally as critically endangered.[6]

---

5.   *Genetic variety* refers to individual differences in offspring caused by differences in DNA passed from parent to offspring.

6.   Dr. Robbin Thorp was a strong advocate for adding both Franklin's bumble bee

As sad as it is to see the rusty-patched bumble bee on endangered species lists, this can ensure the species gets the attention and help it needs. Many scientists keep up-to-date on these lists so they can decide what animals they'll study. Often, we need to learn more about endangered species so we can create helpful conservation efforts, and research by scientists can provide us with the information we need. Endangered species lists help governments make decisions about how land will be used, policies or laws they need to enact, and how they should direct money to support research. Animals that are added to endangered species lists also often get media attention through news articles, which leads to increased public awareness that can inspire people to take action to help save the species. Regular people like us can help by making donations, volunteering our time with citizen science projects like BumbleBeeWatch.org, creating pollinator habitats, or participating in targeted, organized activities, such as fundraising events.

DISTURBING TRENDS

Thanks to Dr. Thorp's early warnings that Franklin's bumble bee was in grave danger, and Dr. Colla and Dr. Packer's efforts in documenting a significant decline in several bumble bee species in Canada and the United States, a number of

---

and the rusty-patched bumble bee to endangered species lists.

scientists began to focus their attention on the status of different bumble bee populations. One such team was led by Dr. Sydney Cameron from the University of Illinois. They designed a gigantic study that involved Dr. Colla and Dr. Packer's strategy of using museum specimens to figure out where different bumble bee species lived over time. They also identified live bumble bees in the field to see where they live today and how big their populations are. Between the years 2007 and 2009, Dr. Cameron's team examined a database that contained a whopping 73,759 records of bumble bee museum specimens from across the United States. They also visited 382 sites across forty states, where they used nets to capture and identify as many bumble bees as they could find. They caught 16,788 bumble bees in total!

When it came time to look at their mountain of data, the team decided to focus on eight bumble bee species. All eight of these species used to be abundant in North America, but scientists had a hunch, based on their observations in the field, that these species were experiencing a shift in their populations. Four species were thought to be declining: the western bumble bee, the American bumble bee, the rusty-patched bumble bee, and the yellow-banded bumble bee. The other four species were suspected to be actually increasing in numbers: the yellow-faced bumble bee (*Bombus vosnesenskii*), the two form bumble bee (*Bombus bifarius*), the two-spotted bumble bee (*Bombus bimaculatus*), and the common eastern bumble bee. What did their data say?

Unfortunately, their suspicions were confirmed. Out of the 16,788 live bumble bees that the team captured across the country, only 532 were the American bumble bee and 129 were the western bumble bee. Things looked particularly bad for the yellow-banded bumble bee and the rusty-patched bumble bee: Only 31 individuals of the yellow-banded had been caught, and only 22 of the rusty-patched. In comparison, they identified 902 individuals of the yellow-faced bumble bee, and thousands of the two form bumble bee, the two-spotted bumble bee, and the common eastern bumble bee. The common eastern came out the winner with the most individuals found.

When the team compared their field data with the records from the huge museum specimen database, they found that the four species that were suspected to be doing well (the yellow-faced bumble bee, two form bumble bee, two-spotted bumble bee, and the common eastern bumble bee) in fact showed no change over time in terms of how widespread they are across the country. For the other four species, however, alarm bells started ringing. Records for the American bumble bee, the western bumble bee, and the yellow-banded bumble bee showed that over the past twenty to thirty years, the area they occupied across the United States shrunk between 23 percent and 30 percent. The range for the rusty-patched shrunk by an incredible 87 percent. It used to be found throughout the eastern United States and the northern Midwest, but in this study, it was only seen at three locations in the state of Illinois and at one site in Indiana. To make matters worse, the team of scientists found that compared to the bumble bee species that seemed to be quite abundant, the declining bumble bee species showed higher levels of infection of the pathogen *N. bombi* and were less genetically diverse, meaning there had probably been inbreeding.

It is clear from all this research that a lot of bumble bee species in North America are in big trouble.

IT'S NOT MUCH BETTER IN THE UNITED KINGDOM . . .

When it comes to bumble bees, things are much different these days compared to the early 1900s when Frederick William Lambert Sladen was diligently watching them, constructing his "humble-bee house," and writing his book. In the 1970s, scientists began to suspect that at least one bumble bee species that was very common during Sladen's time, the ruderal bumble bee, was not around much anymore. By the 1980s, several of the United Kingdom's twenty-seven bumble bee species were suffering: the short-haired bumble bee, the shrill carder bee (*Bombus sylvarum*; see Figure 8-6), the ruderal bumble bee, and the brown-banded carder bee (*Bombus humilis*). Things have become particularly bad for the short-haired bumble bee, since it hasn't been seen anywhere in the United Kingdom since 1988.[7] These days, five more species have disappeared from much of their ranges: the great yellow bumble bee or northern yellow bumble bee (*Bombus distinguendus*; see Figure 8-7), the large carder bee or moss carder bee (*Bombus muscorum*), the broken-belted bumble bee (*Bombus soroeensis*), the red-shanked carder bee (*Bombus rudarius*), and the bilberry bumble bee or mountain bumble bee (*Bombus monticola*).

Nine bumble bee species across the globe are considered vulnerable by the International Union for Conservation of Nature (IUCN), eight species are classified as endangered, and two are critically endangered. The endangered species include the big, beautiful, rusty-colored giant ginger bumble bee, who we met in Chapter Four. The two critically endangered species are the rusty-patched bumble bee and Franklin's bumble bee. Of course, we don't have population information for all 250 bumble bee species around the world. At the time of writing this book, the IUCN Red List only includes 91 species of bumble bees, of which 22 are classified as "Data Deficient," meaning we don't know enough about their numbers yet to know how they're doing.

---

7.   Strangely enough, the short-haired bumble bee and the ruderal bumble bee were two of the species brought to New Zealand from the United Kingdom back in the 1800s (see Chapter One), and they both seem to be doing okay there.

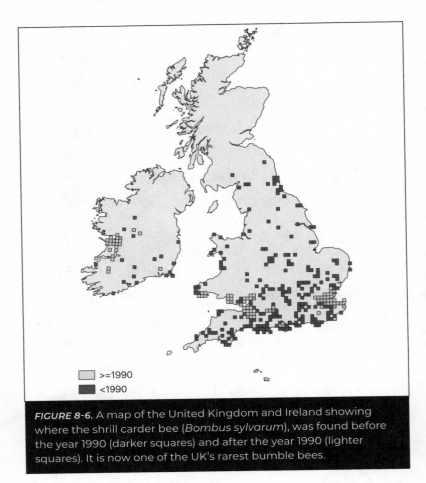

FIGURE 8-6. A map of the United Kingdom and Ireland showing where the shrill carder bee (*Bombus sylvarum*), was found before the year 1990 (darker squares) and after the year 1990 (lighter squares). It is now one of the UK's rarest bumble bees.

WHY ARE SOME BUMBLE BEE SPECIES DOING RATHER WELL?

Among all of this dreadfully bad news, there is one curious thing: Some bumble bee species actually seem to be thriving. For instance, when Dr. Colla and Dr. Packer compared their southern Ontario data to that of the big report done in

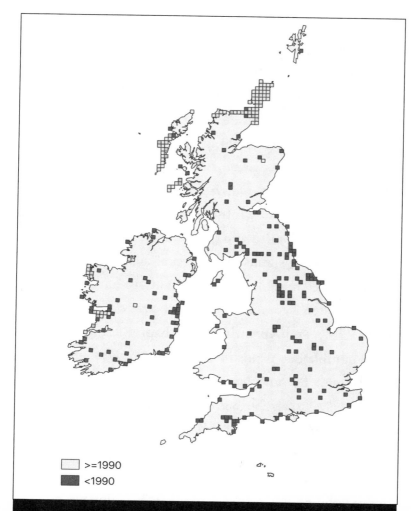

FIGURE 8-7. A map of the United Kingdom and Ireland showing the drastic decline of the great yellow bumble bee (*Bombus distinguendus*). Darker squares are where the bee was found before the year 1990, and lighter squares are where it has been found after 1990. Like the shrill carder bee (Figure 8-6), it's one of the UK's rarest bumble bees.

the 1970s, they discovered that the number of common eastern bumble bees and two-spotted bumble bees had shot up dramatically over time. Similarly, in that giant study across the United States by Dr. Cameron and her team, they found thousands of those same two species, compared to other species that were dwindling. As we saw in Chapter Four, the common eastern bumble bee, which was once found only in eastern North America, has now settled in the west, spreading down from British Columbia, Canada, to Washington State, and potentially, in the future, to California. And we must not forget about the highly adaptable buff-tailed bumble bee, who, thanks to humans importing commercial colonies around the world, has invaded Japan, Chile, and Argentina (see Chapter Four). The buff-tailed bumble bee is pushing out the native species of the large bumble bee and Ezo large bumble bee in Japan, and the giant ginger bumble bee in Chile and Argentina.

So why are some bumble bee species flourishing, while others are floundering? Dr. Dave Goulson, a bumble bee expert in the United Kingdom, has several theories. One is that rare bumble bee species tend to have longer tongues and choose to eat from fewer types of flowers. A lot of the pollen they collect is from plants in the pea, bean, and legume family. The nectar of these plants is often found in deep nectar tubes, which are well suited for long-tongued bumble bees. In the past, the now rare bumble bee species was often seen in grasslands filled with these kinds of plants, but much of these grasslands have since been destroyed to make way for farmland or other human developments. In the remaining grasslands, sometimes fertilizers have been used to boost the growth of grasses for farm animal grazing, but these fertilizers kill off the plants the rare bees love. Destroying these grasslands results in no more food for the long-tongued bees, and likely no more habitat for nesting and hibernation.

On the other hand, more common bumble bee species tend to collect their nectar and pollen from a wide variety of plants, including plants that are not native to the area that are often found in gardens and massive field crops. And if the species has a short tongue and it encounters flowers with a long nectar tube that it can't reach, the species can resort to nectar robbing. The common species, being less picky about what they eat, are not as affected by habitat change. If one food source disappears, they are flexible enough in their food preferences to switch to another source of flowers (if any are available).

Dr. Goulson also thinks that when queen bumble bees emerge from hibernation has something to do with whether a bumble bee species is rare or common. In the United Kingdom at least, there is a strong relationship between when a bumble bee queen emerges in the spring and how rare a species is. Rarer species tend to emerge later in the season. By the time these late-risers are out and about trying to find a place to establish a nest, many nest sites might already be taken by the more common, early-riser bumble bee species. This can especially be a problem if there are fewer nesting sites, for example if humans destroyed some once-popular bumble bee nesting areas. Late-rising, rarer bumble bee species are thus left without a home, spelling death for these queens and their future generations.

Dr. Goulson and other scientists have also noticed that there are major differences between bumble bee species in terms of how far they will fly to find food. The rarer species tend to be doorstep foragers: They often do not fly far from their nest to find flowers. On the other hand, common species such as the buff-tailed bumble bee will fly much farther. In theory, if a bumble bee's foraging range is quite big, this gives it a much better chance to find flowers, especially if areas near the nest are scarce when it comes to bumble-bee-friendly plants. A bigger foraging range would also increase the chances for much more variety in the bumble bee's diet, which contributes to the bumble bee being healthier overall.

It wouldn't be surprising if another factor behind the success of some bumble bee species has to do with genetics. Common species such as buff-tailed bumble bees might have the genes necessary to make it much stronger against a variety of diseases. After all, colonies of buff-tailed bumble bees and common eastern bumble bees are raised in factory-like facilities that can spread infection and disease, and they have managed to survive and thrive for years. Rarer species, such as the giant ginger bumble bee, likely don't have the genetic makeup that allows them to fend off the same infections. Hence their devastating decline.

But just because some bumble bee species are doing well, that doesn't mean we need not worry about the overall fate of bumble bees. If some species become extinct, we can't be sure that the remaining ones will simply pick up the slack. For instance, many of the now rarer bumble bee species appear to be "specialists" for particular native plants. If those bees disappear, those plants may not survive. This can have effects that may not be immediately seen but can be devastating over time: The death of those plants means less food for other animals that eat them, fewer nesting places, and negative effects on soil that may make it more difficult for other plants to grow, which leads to less food for other animals . . . and so on. This might eventually impact what meat and produce are available to us in grocery stores. Dr. Colla provides the example of the rusty-patched and yellow-banded bumble bees. They are among the first to appear when the snow melts. That means their colonies are particularly important to pollinate early blooming fruit plants like blueberries or strawberries. If the yellow-banded bumble bee disappears to the extent the rusty-patched did, those spring blooms may not produce fruit.

The differences between rare and common bumble bee species may be why some of them are beginning to disappear. But there is beauty in the obvious differences that, for example, set the giant ginger bumble bee apart from other bumble bees. There is also beauty in the not-so-obvious differences between bumble bee species that look so similar they have to be distinguished by experts in a laboratory.

As humans, we can appreciate and be aware of the measureless value of the many bumble bee species that exist. Yet more and more, this appreciation needs to include taking action if the variety of species are to survive. As we will see in the next chapter, this action can take many forms. Together, there are so many ways that we can ensure that species such as Franklin's bumble bee and the rusty-patched bumble bee do not vanish forever.

CHAPTER NINE

Hope for Bumble Bees

"So now, somebody has to learn all of the bee songs. Somebody has to learn how to take care of the bees so that they stay. We have to start showing them respect, show them they're important, and make sure that they know."

—Dr. Henry Lickers

SEARCH PARTY

On a beautiful summer morning in 2009 at the University of Stirling in Scotland, the grass glittered with dew and the sun was slowly warming the start to the day. A volunteer search committee stood in a field on the campus grounds, listening to their leader recite instructions. Standing by the leader's side, with a dewy-wet belly and paws, was Toby, a springer spaniel sniffer dog. He was panting, eager to start the search.

The leader, Steph, was a researcher at the university. She launched into the scripted speech that she delivered to every volunteer search committee: what clues to look for; to be careful not to trample on evidence; and finally, as she held up photographs in a binder, how to identify their target.

Steph concluded her instructions, answered several questions from the volunteers, and then everyone fanned out in various directions toward the surrounding woodland. Steph kept Toby on his leash until they were a few feet from the line of trees at the edge of the field. Then she asked Toby to sit. Steph leaned down; commanded, "Find it"; and unclipped the leash from Toby's collar. Nose to the ground, scuttling into the woods this way and that, the dog searched for . . . bumble bee nests.

As Steph explained to the volunteers, bumble bee nests are very tricky to find. Bumble bees tend to choose places hidden from view, such as vacated mouse or vole burrows, among the roots of trees, hedge bottoms, in old logs, under long grass, or anywhere that is dry, dark, and well protected from the rain and wind.

Not only are bumble bee nests hidden from view, but a clear indication of a nest—bumble bee traffic flying into and out of the nest entrance—can be infrequent. This is because bumble bee colonies start off with just a single queen and even at their very peak, the largest nests still only number a few hundred individuals. Traffic in and out of a bumble bee nest is typically one or two bees per minute, as compared to the thousands of individuals that make up a honey bee or wasp nest and the near-constant stream of traffic that gives away their presence.

The search party had their work cut out for them.

Steph asked some of the volunteers to select a space of land and observe it for twenty minutes, whereas she asked other volunteers to walk around and keep an eye to the ground. Toby searched using a zigzagging path.

After a while, Toby lay down on the ground with his snout pointing toward a clump of long grass. Steph walked up, knelt beside Toby, and studied the clump. Sure enough, she heard a low buzzing sound. A black-and-yellow fuzzy worker bumble bee appeared in a tiny space between some grass blades. The bee buzzed her wings and then lifted off, just as Steph identified her as a buff-tailed bumble bee.

"Good boy," Steph said as she took a tennis ball from her pocket and tossed it into Toby's mouth. She wrote down the species of bumble bee, the location of the nest, the date, and time of day.

When the sun was low in the sky, the volunteers trickled in toward the original meeting spot. Steph collected their data sheets. After the last volunteer handed in their sheet, Steph sat down on the grass beside Toby and counted the total number of bumble bee nests that everyone found.

She knew Toby found ten nests: seven nests of buff-tailed bumble bees, one nest of white-tailed bumble bees, one of garden bumble bees, and one of red-tailed bumble bees.

The volunteers who searched by foot found ten nests as well: seven nests of buff-tailed bumble bees, two of white-tailed bumble bees, and one of early bumble bees. The volunteers who watched a fixed area found four nests in total: three nests of buff-tailed bumble bees and one nest of early bumble bees.

Steph carefully slid the data sheets and her clipboard into her backpack. She was eager to calculate how spread out the bumble bee nests were for the search area, but she knew Toby was likely hungry for his dinner. *I'll do the calculations back at the lab*, she thought, as her own stomach grumbled. But she also felt a sinking feeling: Last year a lot more bumble bee nests were found at this time and place.

Why is it important to locate bumble bee nests? Although scientists have been estimating the population size of various species of bumble bees by counting individual worker bees, males, and queens out in the field, a more accurate sense of the size of a bumble bee population can be gained by learning how many nests are in a given area.

We can also more closely study bumble bee biology using wild nests. Although we have learned much about bumble bees, a lot of the research that scientists have done has involved using artificially created colonies. Bumble bee colonies that are bred in captivity may not necessarily be similar to wild colonies. For instance, researchers feed captive colonies as much pollen and nectar as the bees need, especially in the early days of colony development. Wild colonies, on the other hand, have to collect pollen and nectar themselves, and might not have access to the same amounts of pollen and nectar, depending on how many flowers are available at the time of year when the colony is first becoming established. Exposure to more food may place artificial colonies at an advantage compared to wild colonies, as the workers may grow bigger and healthier, which may have an effect on their behavior and survival.

And if we can discover the location of bumble bee nests, this can greatly contribute to conservation efforts. Learning where queen bumble bees choose to build their nests can give us insight into what kind of habitats we can try to provide for them.

It is hoped that detection dogs like Toby can help us find more wild bumble bee nests than we would looking for them on our own. After all, dogs have a much better sense of smell than we do. Over the years, dogs have been trained to recognize and respond to a wide variety of odors. In law enforcement, dogs have been trained to detect explosives, drugs, and missing persons. In conservation efforts, dogs have been trained to sniff out endangered or invasive species.

Research with bumble-bee-nest-detection dogs continued at York University in Toronto, Canada, in the summer of 2019, under the direction of Dr. Sheila Colla (whom we met in Chapter Eight). Together with Amanda Liczner, a student working on her PhD, they tried to locate bumble bee nests in southern Ontario using three dogs from an organization in the United States called Working Dogs for Conservation. Working Dogs for Conservation adopts high-energy dogs from animal shelters and teaches them how to sniff out a variety of important things. These could be destructive weeds, the scat (poop) of endangered animals, and illegal animal products, such as furs and shark fins, that people try to smuggle into different countries. Liczner and Dr. Colla hoped that their Working Dogs, Orbee, Utah, and Tule, could learn how to detect bumble bee nests.

But to find bumble bee nests, the dogs needed examples of wild nests so they would know what they were supposed to look for. Unfortunately, the spring of 2019 in southern Ontario was colder and wetter than usual. The result? Fewer bumble bee queens flying about. It was much harder for Liczner and her team to follow queens to locate their nests for the dogs to smell.[1] Although the team tried giving the

---

1. During spring, one sign of a nest is a queen bumble bee crawling into a hidden space, such as into a small hole in the ground, underneath an object such as a shed, or under a clump of grass.

dogs nest material to sniff, such as wax nectar pots, the dogs still needed actual wild nests to go on. "All three dogs worked at the top of their game," said Alice Whitelaw of Working Dogs for Conservation. But unfortunately, they were unable to locate any bumble bee nests. "Fieldwork is tough!" said Liczner.

FIGURE 9-1. Orbee, who has been with Working Dogs for Conservation since 2009, has helped scientists learn about wolverines, kit foxes, and even gorillas!

Still, the team learned a lot about using dogs to detect nests. "We are going to try to publish a 'lessons learned' guide for using dogs to find bumble bee nests using the information we gathered this year," said Liczner. "Next spring we might try radio-tagging queens to try to follow them back to their nest."

FIGURE 9-2. Utah is one of the newest additions to Working Dogs for Conservation, having joined in 2017. He quickly became an expert in detecting wild kit fox scat, and he helps people monitor the invasive plant Chinese bush clover.

Bumble bee nests are very difficult to find. Between people, dogs, and technology, hopefully one day we can start to locate them more easily. But if that doesn't work, there is always the possibility of providing nests for queen bumble bees to use.

WELCOME TO THE NEST BOX HOTEL

Instead of searching for wild bumble bee nests, some researchers have been

FIGURE 9-3. Tule has been with Working Dogs for Conservation since 2016. So far, she is a specialist in detecting the black-footed ferret.

leaving nest boxes in the wild with the hope that wild bumble bee queens will find them and raise their colonies inside. One of these researchers is Hayley Tompkins, a masters student at the University of Guelph in Canada. She has been placing nest boxes around the province of Ontario each spring and determining how many bumble bee colonies and what species of bumble bees adopt them as their homes. These boxes are modeled after the ones built by Frederick William Lambert Sladen in the early 1900s (we met him in Chapter Two), and basically consist of a plywood box lined with upholsterers' cotton, with a bumble-bee-sized entrance hole (see Figure 9-4). The lids of the wooden boxes are hinged so Hayley and members of her team can lift them up and peek inside to see if the boxes are occupied by bumble bees. The lids are

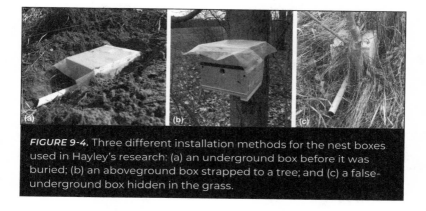

FIGURE 9-4. Three different installation methods for the nest boxes used in Hayley's research: (a) an underground box before it was buried; (b) an aboveground box strapped to a tree; and (c) a false-underground box hidden in the grass.

also covered with waterproof plastic to protect the box from rain.

One aspect of bumble bee nesting behavior that Hayley wants to discover is whether bumble bees have a preference for aboveground nests, underground nests, or "false underground" nests, where the nest is partially covered in long grass or other plants (see Figure 9-4). Maybe different bumble bee species have different preferences?

During the first spring of her research, Hayley installed about four hundred nest boxes across Ontario, in parks, trails, or pockets of land with trees and brush that looked inviting for bumble bees. Thankfully she had a bit of help to construct all those wooden boxes: A local school volunteered to assemble them as a project for their woodshop class. Some of the students even painted them fun colors.

Hayley set up all of the nest boxes in the early spring, when queen bumble bees would be emerging from hibernation, ready to start their nests. Partway through the summer she went back to all the sites and checked each box to see if it was occupied by a bumble bee colony. Then, in the fall, once the new queens and males would have left the nests, mated, and the queens would have buried themselves for the winter while the rest of the bumble bees in the colony would have died off, she collected all of the four hundred nest boxes. When she brought them back to her laboratory, she looked for evidence that a bumble bee colony had lived inside them: dead bumble bee bodies and/or wax structures such as brood cells and nectar pots.

There were several times when Hayley lifted up the lid of one of her nest boxes and was struck with a surprise: mice, snakes, even a salamander. She also discovered some of her underground nest boxes were dug up with big claw marks on them! Another creepy find was when wax moths destroyed a nest. Wax moths are predators of bumble bees, and tend to invade nests near the end of the bumble bee colony cycle. The moths will eat whatever is in the nest and start laying eggs of their own. Sometimes lifting the lid of a box would reveal evidence of a wax-moth-and-bumble bee battle: a bumble bee leg here, a thorax there . . .

In order to try to see the goings-on in a bumble bee nest during the spring and summer, Hayley attached a plumber's snake camera to her smartphone and fed it through the tube leading to an underground nest box she installed. A plumber's snake camera is a tiny camera attached to a long cord, which allows you to see the state of the inside of a pipe: whether it is worn down, damaged, clogged, etc. In Hayley's case, when fed into the inside of an underground nest box, the plumber's camera would allow her to see the bumble bee nest. Hayley knew in which of her underground boxes to insert the camera, because she saw worker bumble bees flying in and out of the entrance tube, meaning there was a bumble bee nest inside. What Hayley didn't anticipate was that "guard bees" were not happy about the intrusion of a camera in their nest! Once, an angry worker bee chased the camera down the tube as Hayley pulled it up (Hayley could watch the bee running along the tube on her phone screen), and when the bee arrived at the entrance of the tube, she chased Hayley away!

Eerie discoveries and surprises aside, what has Hayley found from her research? Do bumble bees use her boxes for their nests? And do they have a preference for aboveground nests, underground nests, or partially covered nests?

Out of the four hundred nest boxes that Hayley placed all over Ontario, she found that about forty of them were chosen by wild bumble bee queens to establish their nests. So, there was about a 10 percent occupation rate. A variety of different bumble bee species made the boxes their home, with most choosing the aboveground nests that were strapped to trees or poles. A small number of bumble bee queens chose the underground nests, but none of the partially covered nests were chosen. One exciting finding was that two colonies of the half-black bumble bee—a species that typically nests at or below the ground—chose to make their home in Hayley's aboveground boxes. This means that wild bumble bees might be flexible in where they choose to nest.

If we provide more artificial nesting sites like Hayley has been doing, perhaps bumble bee queens will have a much easier time finding a home, especially considering how much natural habitat has been—and is being—destroyed by humans. But scientists have also been taking a number of other steps to try to study and conserve bumble bee species, including throwing parties!

A SURPRISE GUEST AT A POLLINATOR PARTY

Dr. Elaine Evans sat in the shade at a picnic table in Lyndale Park in Minneapolis, Minnesota. She could hear the faint sound of live music in the distance. There was a slight scent of food in the air. It was the day of the Pollinator Party that she had worked so hard to organize. She hoped that the music and food were attracting a large crowd. For now, Dr. Evans had to wait at her picnic table for her group of citizen scientists to return with what she hoped was a large number of various bumble bee species they found on their hike.

Dr. Evans had planned the Pollinator Party to raise public awareness about honey bees, wild bees such as bumble bees, and their importance in producing the food we eat. Besides being a festival with educational activities about pollinators, people could volunteer to become citizen scientists and go on a walk around the park to look for bumble bees. Dr. Evans gave these volunteers small, cup-sized plastic containers with a lid and asked them to try to capture any bumble bees they saw. The volunteers then brought them back to the picnic table where Dr. Evans was waiting, and she identified the species of bumble bee they found.

During the Pollinator Party, Dr. Evans took careful notes on how many bumble bees were captured, what species they were, and, if possible, the type of flower on which they were found. Dr. Evans planned to enter this data into the Minnesota Bumble Bee Survey, which is a project monitoring long-term changes in bumble bee communities in parks in the Twin Cities of Minneapolis and St. Paul. It helps scientists like Dr. Evans see how bumble bee communities change over the decades, track remaining populations of endangered bees, and keep an eye on the health of other species. So, just as Dr. Evans intended, the Pollinator Party served two important purposes: It allowed for much more bumble bee data to be collected for the survey than Dr. Evans could do on her own, and it was an opportunity for the volunteers to learn about bumble bees and their struggle to survive. In the process, she hoped people would gain a new respect for bumble bees, too.

"Dr. Evans, I found a bee!"

Dr. Evans turned to see a girl in a butter-colored T-shirt and bright green shorts skipping down the path toward her. She was holding one of the containers Dr. Evans had handed out to the volunteers. The girl's mother was walking close behind her.

"Let's have a look," said Dr. Evans as the girl handed her the container. Dr. Evans held it up at eye level and peered at the bumble bee that was buzzing and bouncing around inside. "This is *Bombus impatiens*, the common eastern bumble bee. She's a nice, plump worker bee. Great job!"

Dr. Evans wrote the information on the data sheet on her clipboard. Then she opened the container inside a butterfly net and set the worker bee free inside the net. Grasping sections of the net, she very carefully cornered the bee into a small area. Then she took out her paint pen and dabbed a tiny dot of bright orange, nontoxic paint onto the mesh of the net, which seeped onto the bee's thorax. That way, the volunteers would see that that bee had already been counted. Then she set the bumble bee free.

All of the volunteers slowly started to make their way back. Dr. Evans was delighted to see that everybody carried a container with a bumble bee inside.

"That's a *Bombus fervidus*, the golden northern bumble bee."

"Here we have *Bombus griseocollis*, the brown-belted bumble bee."

"And this is *Bombus bimaculatus*, the two-spotted bumble bee."

One by one Dr. Evans identified the bees, marked the data on her sheets, dabbed the bees with paint, and set them free.

A boy in a blue baseball cap stepped up and held out his container. "Look! My bee has a brown splotch on its back."

Dr. Evans's heart skipped a beat as she took the container from the boy. She peered inside.

"It's . . . it's *Bombus affinis*! The rusty-patched bumble bee!" She stared at the bee's fur pattern again to make sure she was correct. Indeed, it was a rusty-patched. "This is an excellent find," she told the boy. "The rusty-patched bumble bee is endangered and not seen very often in the wild anymore. This is a nice, healthy worker bee, which means that somewhere out there, there is a whole colony of rusty-patched bumble bees!"

"I used to be afraid of bees," said the boy, "but now they are my favorite animal."

A while after the Pollinator Party came to an end, to her surprise, Dr. Evans saw rusty-patched bumble bees now and then in the parks she surveys, and even in her own yard. But the rusty-patched is still in danger. Its range has shrunk drastically. (Recall from Chapter Eight that it hasn't been seen in Canada since 2009.) The small population that is left could suffer from inbreeding, which could lead to health problems and/or males who cannot mate. The species would no longer be able to create new colonies, leading to its extinction.

Still, sightings of rusty-patched bumble bees like Dr. Evans's are cause for hope that the species can make a comeback. The US Fish and Wildlife Service is creating a recovery plan for the rusty-patched. Hopefully their recovery plan won't come too late to save the species. In the meantime, if you live in areas where the rusty-patched has been found, Wildlife Preservation Canada suggests planting the native flowers listed below to help support the bees' survival throughout its colony life.

Spring	Early Summer
Atlantic camas	Bee balm
Dutchman's breeches	Blackberry
Eastern waterleaf	Pinnate prairie coneflower
Pussy willow	Red columbine
Virginia bluebells	Smooth rose
	Swamp milkweed

Late Summer	Fall
Canada goldenrod	Calico aster
Dwarf larkspur	Handsome Harry
Purple prairie clover	Leafcup
Spotted joe-pye weed	Marsh hedgenettle
Woodland sunflower	New England aster

Dr. Evans also suggests the following things you can do to help the rusty-patched, or any other species of bumble bee: "The bees need places to nest. Leaving some messy corners in your yard with piles of leaves or sticks can help. Also, keep flowers for bees free of pesticides."

"People are used to endangered species being exotic creatures in remote places," Dr. Evans adds. "With the rusty-patched bumble bee, our gardens and our parks are their homes."

But there *are* also bumble bees suffering in far-off places. Some scientists, like Dr. Amy Toth, have traveled to these areas in hopes of helping those bees, too.

SAVING THE GIANT GINGER BUMBLE BEE

Dr. Amy Toth's backpack began to feel heavy. Her hiking shoes felt tight on her feet after a day of searching. She trudged through the long grass, trying not to feel discouraged. *At least it's a beautiful day*, she told herself. *I'm in Argentina, and I'm doing what I love.* She took a deep breath of the cool, clean air and looked out into the distance. The park seemed so immense. *We will find them eventually.*

She looked up, scanned the distance, and saw something that triggered a surge of hope: an abandoned apple orchard. "Look, Eduardo!" She pointed at the brilliant white, blossoming trees. "There must be bees there!"[2]

They both picked up their pace and headed for the trees. As they approached, Dr. Toth could hear the collective hum

---

2. Although I quote Amy speaking English, as part of her year in Argentina, she practiced her Spanish with Eduardo and the rest of her research group.

of buzzing bees. She stopped at the base of one tree and scanned the cloud of fragrant blooms. There were numerous buff-tailed bumble bee queens buzzing around from flower to flower, with their distinctive yellow-and-black banding and whitish-tan rear end. So far, over the course of the day, Dr. Toth had counted almost two hundred of the invasive buff-tails at Nahuel Huapi National Park, and no native giant ginger bumble bees at all. In fact, she had yet to see any giant gingers since she started her fieldwork in Argentina.

Then she heard it: a low, loud, huge buzz. She knew exactly what it was. "It's here somewhere, Eduardo! There's a giant ginger queen!"

Later, Dr. Toth told me that you hear giant ginger bumble bee queens before you see them. "Their buzz is like nothing else I've ever heard."

Dr. Toth scanned the tree. Then she saw it.

"They're just bright

FIGURE 9-5. The first giant ginger bumble bee queen that Dr. Amy Toth encountered on her year-long research trip to Argentina. The queen is feeding on an apple blossom.

orange," Dr. Toth recalled. "They kind of pop out at you. They're like these flying buses. They don't look like they should be able to fly. They're kind of clumsy. I've studied a lot of species before and I had never really seen something that big and airborne!

"And their fur is just so thick and dense," she continued. "They kind of have this mammal-like appearance. You want to pet them because they look so plush."

Dr. Eduardo Zattara raised his camera and snapped a few pictures of the big orange bee. With a quick flick of her wrist, Dr. Toth caught it in her butterfly net. She placed the net on the grass and then managed to capture the queen in a small, clear, plastic tube. Dr. Zattara opened their small cooler and Dr. Toth gently placed the tube inside it, between two ice packs. After closing the lid, they waited for a few minutes for the queen to fall asleep.

Once the giant ginger queen was snoozing, Dr. Toth and Dr. Zattara got to work. They knew they only had about ten minutes before the queen would start waking up, so they packed as many measurements and observations as they could into that small length of time. First, Dr. Toth took a small pair of micro scissors and clipped off one of the rear tarsus of the bee (see Figure 9-6). It was like clipping off a teeny-tiny piece of its foot: The bee would still be able to walk and move around like normal.[3] She put the tiny piece

---

3.   Since animals cannot tell us with words that they are in pain, we look for any behaviors or sounds they make that show they are suffering. After a piece of tarsus is clipped from a bumble bee's leg and it wakes up, the bumble bee acts as if nothing happened, so we assume the bee is not feeling pain.

of tarsus into a little tube and put it on ice, so that she could bring it back to her lab at Iowa State University and study its DNA.[4]

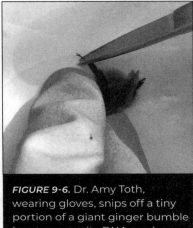

FIGURE 9-6. Dr. Amy Toth, wearing gloves, snips off a tiny portion of a giant ginger bumble bee tarsus so its DNA can be examined.

Dr. Toth is an expert in genetics,[5] and no genetic work has been done yet on the giant ginger bumble bee. She hopes to collect samples from a number of individuals of the species so that she can determine whether, because of its dwindling population, the bees have less genetic diversity. This would mean the species is becoming inbred, and thus less able to ward off disease and other health issues. If the giant ginger bumble bee population in Argentina is indeed suffering from a lack of genetic diversity, we may be able to start introducing individuals from Chile, where they are a bit more abundant, to Argentina to add a little more genetic variety

---

4. To study DNA, you need some kind of sample from the individual you want to examine, like skin or other body tissue. Taking a teeny piece of a bumble bee's tarsus is the least harmful way to get a tissue sample from a bee.

5. *Genetics* is a branch of biology focused on how organisms inherit traits from their parents. It's all about DNA (deoxyribonucleic acid) and genes, variety, and heredity.

to the country's species. The species would then have a much better chance of survival.

Because the giant ginger bumble bee is becoming quite rare, and we know very little about the species, when Dr. Toth found one of these big, beautiful bees, she took full advantage of the ten minutes while the bee was asleep and measured everything she possibly could. She measured the width of its head and the size of its thorax, she noted what type of plant the bee was feeding on, and she also took a picture of its wings to determine how worn they were (see Figure 9-7).

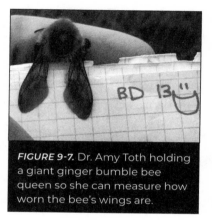

FIGURE 9-7. Dr. Amy Toth holding a giant ginger bumble bee queen so she can measure how worn the bee's wings are.

"The wings tell a story about the bee's age and experience," Dr. Toth explained later. "Several studies on different species of bees and wasps have shown a very strong relationship between basically the number of miles flown and how tattered the wings are. I was just giving them a score from zero to four: perfect to completely destroyed. It would be kind of interesting if [at] sites where they're more abundant, for example, they don't have to work as hard to get their food, so their wings aren't quite as beat up."

After Dr. Toth and Dr. Zattara took all their measurements, they put a little dab of paint on the queen's leg so that if they encountered her again, they would know that she'd already been studied. They were just in time, too, as the queen was writhing and almost fully awake. Dr. Toth and Dr. Zattara watched her for a few seconds, and then the giant ginger bee lifted off and flew up toward the apple tree, free to forage and live in the wild once again.

Dr. Toth stayed in Argentina for a full year to study the giant ginger bumble bee. As spring flowed into summer, and summer shifted to fall, she was able to observe queens, workers, and males of the species as wild colonies passed through their cycle. In some areas she found more of the bees than others, and some days she came back with empty data sheets, having seen no giant ginger bees at all. Often in those cases she saw plenty of the invasive buff-tailed bumble bee, though.

But there were a number of memorable moments out in the field that made up for the days when giant ginger bumble bees were scarce. Besides the thrill of finding her first queen, later in the

FIGURE 9-8. Dr. Amy Toth in the field holding Fidel, a male giant ginger bumble bee they captured five times on the same plant.

year Dr. Toth captured the
same giant ginger male on
five separate occasions over
three weeks, on the exact
same plant![6] A dot of paint
they had placed on his leg
during his first capture
allowed them to identify
him later. They just had to
name him, so they called
him Fidel (see Figures 9-8
and 9-9).

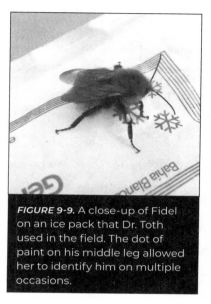

FIGURE 9-9. A close-up of Fidel on an ice pack that Dr. Toth used in the field. The dot of paint on his middle leg allowed her to identify him on multiple occasions.

And these bumble bees
grew on Dr. Toth. "The vast majority of my work has not
been on bumble bees, actually," she said later. "It's been on
honey bees and on paper wasps.[7] I just kind of became fascinated with the story of the giant ginger bumble bee, and the
decline was just so striking, and it just called out to me. They
need help. This bee needs help. And it's happening right
now. The decline is before our very eyes and I feel like it's

---

6.   After leaving the nest, male bumble bees choose and patrol a specific space of
land where they hope to encounter queen bumble bees to mate with. Finding a male
bumble bee so many times at the same spot suggests he was quite loyal to his territory!

7.   *Paper wasps* are large, flying, stinging insects. They make their nests by gathering fibers from dead wood and plant stems and mixing it with their saliva. The result
is a gray or brown papery structure. Like bumble bees, paper wasps live in colonies
with a queen and workers.

something that if you could get the right information quickly, you could do something about it. And so, I've become obsessed with this bee! Especially now that I've seen them and chased them and seen them in action. They're just beautiful. They're stunning. They're big, they're furry, they're the perfect icon for insect conservation in a lot of ways. And I thought, *Maybe I can do something that could help.* That's what got me into it."

So, after all of her fieldwork and data gathering in Argentina, has Dr. Toth gained any insights into the cause or causes of the drastic decline of the giant ginger bumble bee? She hasn't analyzed all of her information yet, but what she sees so far gives us some clues. For instance, she measured the body size of all the giant ginger bumble bees she captured. She expected that in areas where she found lots of giant ginger bees, their body size would be bigger compared to giant ginger bees found in areas where there were fewer bees. This is because if there are more giant ginger bees in a spot, there must be lots of food to go around in that area, so their lives are easier, and so they must be bigger in size. But it turns out the body size of the bees were similar no matter where they came from. So, the amount of food that is available to the bees does not appear to explain why the giant ginger bumble bee is disappearing.

However, Dr. Toth compared the body measurements of the giant ginger bees she took in the field with museum specimens of the species she found in the Bernardino Rivadavia Natural Sciences Museum in Buenos Aires. The museum specimens were collected before the invasion of buff-tailed bumble bees. She did find that giant ginger queens seemed to be larger before the buff-tails took over. This means that perhaps there is not quite as much food to go around for all the bees, and so the giant ginger bumble bee is not growing as large as it has in the past.

But the best explanation so far as to why the giant ginger bumble bee is suffering? A parasite. Dr. Toth's partners in Argentina, Dr. Marina Arbetman, Dr. Carolina Morales, and Dr. Marcelo Aizen, suspected commercial colonies of buff-tailed bumble bees that were imported into Chile for pollinating crops carried the *Apicystis bombi* parasite (*A. bombi* for short), which doesn't seem to affect that species. But the team found evidence that *A. bombi* spread to giant ginger bumble bees, which would never have faced the parasite before and thus wouldn't have had a chance to build up any immunity to it. Dr. Morales documented that wherever buff-tails started to appear, there was a large, rapid decline in giant ginger bees. She worked hard with her team to get the species "Red listed" on the IUCN list of endangered species.

A deadly parasite could definitely explain the quick disappearance of the ginger giant. "There could be other diseases, too," added Dr. Toth. The team of Dr. Arbetman,

Dr. Morales, Dr. Aizen, and Dr. Zattara just received a new grant from the National Geographic Foundation to look at disease in bees. Dr. Toth will be helping them collect bees and do DNA analyses. "Our research will actually be focused on buff-tails rather than the giant ginger bee," said Dr. Toth, "because with giant ginger bees, you can't really find them. You can't really do much." The plan is to map out all of the genetics of the diseases that buff-tailed bumble bees carry. They will look at these genetics over time and across different locations to see if the diseases change. Dr. Toth and her team predict that as time passes, we should see more and more variety in the diseases that buff-tails are bringing, since diseases can grow and change. "All of this gets to what we want to accomplish with the research," said Dr. Toth, "which is to find actual hard evidence that continuing to import buff-tails to Chile is harming the giant ginger bumble bee."

Many people continue to import buff-tails into Chile anyway because they see them everywhere, so they believe the damage has already been done. They think, *What's the harm in bringing in a few more colonies?* But Dr. Toth points out that every time a new colony of buff-tails is brought into Chile from Europe, it could be slightly genetically different from the colonies of buff-tails already in Chile. This means the new bees might be better at fighting off disease or be better able to cope with challenges in their new environment.

In other words, they are making the invader stronger. Plus, new colonies could have a disease that the giant ginger bumble bee has never experienced before.

But it's just a bee, people may think. *It's a beneficial insect so we'll bring it into our country.* What they fail to realize is that every place in the world already has insects, birds, bats, or other animals that pollinate plants. "Almost every place you go there are hundreds of species of native bees," Dr. Toth points out. "We could harness that power, that pollination power that's already there for free, to help with the crops that we love."

Dr. Toth plans on returning to Argentina in the near future to continue her field research on the giant ginger bee and the buff-tailed bumble bee. In the meantime, she has piles of data to analyze from her most recent trip to try to discover clues for how to help save the lovable ginger giant.

A SCIENTIST WISH LIST

The continuing research and efforts of scientists such as Hayley Tompkins, Dr. Elaine Evans, Dr. Amy Toth, Dr. Sheila Colla (whom we met in Chapter Eight), and new methods such as using detection dogs to "sniff out" bumble bee nests, provide us with the information we need to make smart decisions about bumble bee conservation efforts. There are many, many other scientists around the world (some of whom we met in previous chapters) who study bumble bees and who are making very meaningful contributions to that end. A number of them (such as the late Dr. Robbin Thorp, whom we also met in Chapter Eight) have worked tirelessly to ensure that the species that are in trouble are added to endangered species lists so the bees can get the attention they need. In a way, worldwide, there exists an army of scientists in the battle to save the bumble bees.

But there is much, much more work to be done. Richard Hatfield, who is a bumble bee conservation scientist at the Xerces Society for Invertebrate Conservation, points out that we're still guessing about basic things such as where bumble bees nest, how far species are distributed, and where they are vulnerable. But beyond basic biological questions, Hatfield, like many other scientists, has a wish list of what he'd like to see happen when it comes to protecting bumble bees. One of the top things on his list is to get a list of clear rules, based on evidence, about when and how much people can use pesticides that are toxic to bees and other animals. "Currently, farmers, homeowners, anyone really in the United States, can use pesticides whether they really need to or not," he said. The way people use them so far is causing contamination of the environment and is harming pollinators such as wild bees. Of course, not using toxic pesticides at all would be ideal. "A complete ban of some of these chemicals is something I would support," said Hatfield, "but I don't think we'll get there anytime soon in the US. Generally, pesticides should be a last resort, not a first line of defense. There are other things we can do first, such as creating healthy lands that can fend off pests naturally."

Hatfield also hopes for more rules for breeding, selling, and keeping bees. That means new rules for both commercial bumble bees and honey bees. "There's a lot of evidence that commercial bumble bees were responsible for spreading and amplifying the disease that led to the decline of the rusty-patched bumble bee," said Hatfield. "But there's also a lot of evidence that honey bees, who are not native to North America, are competing with and also spreading diseases to native bees. So, at the bare minimum, we should be tracking the use of commercial pollinators, where they are being used, and to what extent."

As we saw in Chapter Four, commercial bumble bees escaping from greenhouses has been a huge problem. Wild bees can suffer when the escaped bees take over land and spread disease. For example, the only species currently available commercially in North America is the common eastern bumble bee, which lives in the wild east of the Rocky Mountains. But it is shipped all over the continent without regard to its potential effects on the native species. Hatfield hopes that in the future commercial bumble bees will be used within their native range and not shipped outside of it. Hatfield also hopes for regulations that ensure that commercial bumble bees are only used for greenhouse pollination (as opposed to pollination in open fields), and then ensuring that those greenhouses are properly screened to keep the commercial bees inside, and keep the wild bees outside.

We could even create another level of protection by allowing a group of people who are not involved in any commercial bee companies to test bumble bee colonies for diseases before they are shipped out of the companies. The honey bee industry actually does this to some degree already. Some states in the United States have rules that if you are going to bring in honey bees from outside of the state, they have to pass an inspection from an independent inspection group that they are free from mites and disease. But, Hatfield pointed out, "With bumble bees I'm not sure we actually even know what diseases we're looking for. There's a lot we don't understand, and likely there are diseases that haven't been identified yet. I don't think we understand enough about the pathology of these animals to make sure we can protect them by disease inspections alone."[8]

Genevieve Rowe, lead biologist at Wildlife Preservation Canada's Native Pollinator Initiative, mentions that the work that bumble bee scientists—like the ones we've met in this book—are doing is making a difference, but changes to

---

8.   *Pathology* is the study of diseases: where they come from, how they develop, what they do to living things, and how we can get rid of them.

regulations that are based on their research may take time to be put into action. Scientists like Ms. Rowe collect and review data so they can make recommendations for governments and the public on how to protect species at risk of extinction. It often takes a while for these recommendations to be put into action, but not necessarily because the policy makers disagree with the scientists. It takes a while because it takes time for new rules to be put into place, and for people to learn how they can change their behavior to make a positive impact. Ms. Rowe knows a lot of scientists have been doing tons of work to measure the health of bumble bee species in Canada, and as a result, she believes that we will see more recommendations from these scientists being put into play in the near future. This can all be a part of recovery plans that governments develop to help species at risk.

One thing the Xerces Society has been pushing to regulate is the movement of commercial bumble bees across the United States—one of Hatfield's wish list items. Sarina Jepsen, one of Hatfield's colleagues at the Xerces Society and also a conservation scientist, is among the team members who has pushed for laws that limit the movement of commercial bumble bee colonies. "We basically felt like we hit a wall, like there was nothing more that we could do," she said. "We tried proactively urging the US Fish and Wildlife Agency. First, they said they had no authority. Then they came back and said, 'Okay, we do have the authority to regulate, but we just don't have the capacity.' It's really hard to get agencies to regulate." As Jepsen suggested, new and creative ideas are needed in order to get regulations put in place.

There are things on the scientist wish list for protecting bumble bees that the public can help with, however. For instance, Dr. Sheila Colla does a lot of outreach work. She finds that with all of the media attention given to honey bees, there is a common misunderstanding that saving honey bees is a way to save bumble bees. So some people might start raising their own honey bee hives in their backyard in an attempt to "save the bees." But this could actually introduce disease to native pollinators and create competition for food. What regular people can do is be selective about what we plant in our gardens. "There's this whole argument that if you plant plants for honey bees, you can support other pollinators as well," said Dr. Colla. "But honey bees take a lot of resources out of a system. Honey bees store food for the wintertime, so they take more pollen and nectar. Native bees, on the other hand, sleep over the winter, so they don't need to store honey. And honey bee colonies are so large that they'll take more resources for that reason as well."

If you want to plant flowers, Dr. Colla suggests avoiding seeds that are advertised as "bee-friendly flowers," unless they are flowers that are native to your area. "General 'bee-friendly flowers' that are sold across the country are not native to every area in the country," Dr. Colla explained. "Each species of bee has their own preferences for what grows naturally in their area. So, it's best to plant native flowers. And make sure you have plants blooming all the way from the spring to the fall." This ensures that all stages of the bumble bee life cycle are supplied with food: from the queens that emerge in spring to the worker bees during summer and to the new queens and males in fall.

Besides planting more native flowers, there is another important thing that regular people can do to help wild bumble bees: participate in citizen science.

THE RISE OF CITIZEN SCIENCE

Around the year 2008, Richard Hatfield and Dr. Sheila Colla were working together on conservation efforts for the rusty-patched bumble bee. Hatfield is based in the Portland, Oregon, office of the Xerces Society. Dr. Colla is based in Canada. At the time they had students and staff doing fieldwork, looking for the rusty-patched bumble bee, but they realized there were only so many students and staff who could take time to do this, and their teams could only be in one place at a time. How could they increase their chances of spotting the rusty-patched in areas where it used to be found, if it was indeed out there, and get a truer sense of how the species was doing?

Hatfield and Dr. Colla had an idea. They asked people to take pictures of any rusty-patched bumble bee they saw and email the photos to them, including details such as the date and location where the bee was seen. That way they could have a much larger network of people over a larger area looking for the rusty-patched. And it worked! Emails started flowing in.

But something interesting happened. Although people were asked to send photos of the rusty-patched bumble bee, about 90 percent of what Hatfield and Dr. Colla received were not pictures of the rusty-patched at all, but other, more common bumble bee species! Sometimes, for people who are not used to identifying bumble bees, it is very tricky to correctly identify the species of a bumble bee, given that they can have very subtle differences in color patterns. This was turning out to be the case with the rusty-patched.

Hatfield and Dr. Colla realized that between the two of them, they couldn't keep up with the number of emails that were coming in. But if they decided to enter into their database only true sightings of the rusty-patched and any other rare species of bumble bee emailed to them, it would make these rare species look more common than they actually were. With their already busy work schedules, how could they keep up with all the incoming emails and include all of the bee sightings without falling behind?

That was in 2008. By 2014, they had teamed up with organizations that could help, such as the University of Ottawa, the Montreal Insectarium, the Natural Museum in London, and BeeSpotter at the University of Illinois. They also asked for, and received, financial support from a long list of organizations who were interested in supporting their plans. As a result, their project began to transform. Instead of having to enter each bumble bee sighting themselves, the Xerces Society and Dr. Colla created an online platform where the public can upload photos of their bumble bee sightings, enter their own data, and, with online pictures and descriptions to help guide them, try to identify the species of bumble bee they found. A large number of bumble bee experts from across North America volunteered to help verify the identities of the bumble bees in the submitted photos.

BumbleBeeWatch.org was born.

By five years later, in 2019, over thirty-eight thousand photos of bumble bees had been uploaded to the site. And the sightings continue to pour in. "The response has been way more than any of us anticipated," said Hatfield. "That's something that gives you hope for the rusty-patched and other bumble bee species: all these people who are spending time to go onto the site and provide information."

Hatfield is also hopeful about regular people's interest

in bumble bees. "I've been working on bumble bee conservation for over twenty years now," he said. "When I first started, if I was going to give a workshop about bumble bee conservation, one or two people might have showed up. Now, I can't get a venue big enough! I recently hosted an event in Portland and there were a hundred people in the room. It was sold out, and people were waiting outside hoping to get in. I think people want to do the right thing and they just want to know how to help. That's one of the most hopeful things: that people care, and they want to make a difference.

"One of the greatest things we can do," he said, "is to realize that we have a safari in our backyards and parks. Almost anywhere in North America there's ten to fifteen species of bumble bees that could be there. Wildlife watching and conservation doesn't have to involve big, furry mammals. It can be a small furry bee in your backyard."

Sarina Jepsen agrees. People might not feel much of a connection with the birds, amphibians, and large mammals that are on endangered species lists. But a listed bumble bee is in people's backyards. "With an insect species," Ms. Jepsen said, "a lot of people can actually be part of the solution and really feel like they are part of the solution. If they're within the range of the species, there are some really simple things that people can do, such as plant a garden, not use pesticides, and create a home for the endangered species. That's a really cool thing. I think it's hard to find a parallel with other endangered species where individuals can help the species directly and maybe even have a chance of providing habitat and having it come into their own backyard or parks."

Ms. Jepsen also made the point that smartphones, the internet, and technology in general are really changing the way people send, receive, and process information. There is a lot of hope and potential for how current and future technology can help people learn about native species, conservation, and what the public can do to help. Maybe BumbleBeeWatch.org is just the beginning of a future where scientists and citizen scientists come together to protect our wonderful variety of wild bumble bee species across the planet. Who knows what the young people of today will end up inventing that will change and improve the way we undertake conservation efforts?

Something similar to BumbleBeeWatch.org is being used to track the giant ginger bumble bee. Salvemos Nuestro Abejorro (Save Our Bumble Bee) is an organization led by bumble bee expert Jose Montalva. People in Chile and Argentina can upload photographs of the giant ginger bee or the invasive buff-tailed bumble bee to the organization's website, along with the date and location where the bee was seen. In addition to helping scientists track the status of the critically endangered species, this can help locate pockets of the bee's population that might be hidden in remote areas.

Over in the United Kingdom, an organization called the Bumblebee Conservation Trust leads a number of projects to track and conserve various bumble bee species. One of their public projects is BeeWalk. BeeWalk involves volunteers (called BeeWalkers) who walk the same route (called a transect) at least once a month from March to October. This time frame covers from when queens emerge from hibernation to when worker bees are flying around for food, and finally to when males and new queens appear. Each BeeWalker is assigned an area that is roughly thirteen feet by seven feet, and they record the number of each bumble bee species they see there. Between 2008 and 2018, there were over 120,000 records submitted to BeeWalk! And the program continues to expand across the UK. All of this volunteer work has greatly helped scientists understand how the various UK bumble bee species are doing nationwide.

The hundreds of people who continue to show up to Hatfield's presentations on native bees, the thousands of bumble bee sightings submitted to BumbleBeeWatch.org, and the enthusiastic efforts of BeeWalkers show that there are a lot of regular people out there who want to help wild bumble bees with their struggle to survive, and who want to preserve a beautiful and important animal on this planet. What is also very exciting is that citizen science efforts such as BumbleBeeWatch.org, Salvemos Nuestro Abejorro, and BeeWalk are still rather new. There is much potential for them to grow and develop, and to inspire people to develop other ways that we can do conservation work. With more people—including you!—spreading the word about what bumble bees are, how bumble bees need our help, and what we can do about their suffering, this might be only the beginning of a global wave of change to make sure we don't lose our tiny furry friends who support and provide so much life on Earth.

THE GOOD NEWS

The relationship between humans and bumble bees has been a complex one, to say the least. Indigenous people respected them, passed down traditional knowledge about bumble bees through generations, and lived alongside bumble bees peacefully. Peoples who focused on agriculture enjoyed an especially mutually beneficial relationship with bumble bees: they grew native plants to feed their people, which provided bumble bees with food as well.

Then folks started traveling the globe. The human population started to increase. More and more people needed to be fed. With good intentions, people moved bumble bees across continents and began breeding them at a massive scale, to take advantage of their pollination power. Land rich with a variety of wildflowers and native plants, which sustained bumble bees for hundreds of years before humans came along, was gradually replaced with cities and vast fields of only one type of food crop. Pesticides were invented. Bee diseases spread. Thanks to a variety of human activities, things now look pretty bleak for many bumble bee species. The bond that humans and bumble bees once had has, in many ways, vanished. It is now very much a one-sided relationship where humans take and take from bumble bees and don't give back, to the point that humans are destroying the species.

But then we have people such as Charles Darwin, Frederick William Lambert Sladen, and a massive number of scientists, many of whom you've met in these pages, who strive to understand bumble bees. They are curious about their basic biology, like where they choose to establish their nests, or about their inner worlds, such as their complex problem-solving abilities, their ability to picture shapes in their head or feel emotions. And many members of the public are interested in bumble bees, too—hopefully including you!

These regular people and bee experts are seeing the exploitation of bumble bees for what it is. They see that humans are turning fields of wildflowers that were once crucial sources of food and habitat for bees into single-crop wastelands or concrete cities, roads, and houses. They see that pesticides are poisoning whatever lands are left for bees to feed from and live in, whether it's a field of flowering crops or a perfectly kept garden or front lawn. And now they also need to see the damage being done by shipping bumble bees all over the globe. These people want to do something about it. And many of them *are* doing something about it, in their own ways.

Just like any relationship can change, our relationship with bumble bees can change. We can have hope that it can change for the better, and we can act on that hope. Humans have ignored the bee song for many, many years. But that doesn't mean we can't start listening to their songs now. If we start to listen, what would their songs be about? Perhaps bumble bees are singing that you need to open your eyes, that they need your help, but you can change things for the better. Perhaps, if we listen, they are singing that it's not too late to aim and strive for a peaceful, balanced existence with them once again.

Author's Note

I'm not sure why you picked up this book. Maybe the title sparked your interest. Maybe you love animals and wanted to learn more about bumble bees in particular. Maybe you heard about bees in the news. Or maybe it was assigned reading for a class and you were forced to read it! Whatever your reason or reasons may be, I want to thank you. I hope I was able to convince you to feel at least a little more fondness toward those plump, fuzzy creatures that buzz from flower to flower.

One thing I hope I didn't do was make you feel discouraged about the future. I know I wrote a lot about diseases and pesticides and the dwindling numbers of many bumble bee species. I have to admit, researching and writing all of the bad news made me feel quite depressed about the state of things. But at the same time, I decided I had to include those topics because they are very important chapters in the story of humans and bumble bees. I wanted to tell you the truth, and the truth is that things don't look all that good. At the same time, I wanted to end the book with some hope. And I was delighted to find that there *is* a lot of hope.

It would break my heart to have you read this book and then feel that it is entirely up to you, the younger generation, to solve all of our environmental problems. It is not fair to place the responsibility of "saving the bees" on your shoulders. Some of you might feel like you *do* want to tackle our environmental problems. You feel passionate about climate change or species conservation or whatever, and you want to make it your life's work, and you want to be our leaders. And that's wonderful! We desperately need people like you! But we're not all like that.

What I would like to do if your passions happen to lie somewhere else (which is a good thing—we need variety in the world) is leave you with a feeling that you *can* do something. It can be a big something or a little something, whatever you feel confident doing. Want to convince your parents to leave an old pile of leaves in the corner of the backyard so that a queen bumble bee might make her nest there? Great! Want to hang a little flower planter box outside your apartment window with native plants that wild bumble bees will visit? Fantastic! Or perhaps if you are more outgoing, you could talk to your neighbors or even city leaders about why they use pesticides on their lawns and the benefits to the environment if they *don't* use pesticides. Let the dandelions grow so the bees have food early in the spring! You can talk to your teachers about starting a wildflower garden for bees on your school property.

Here's a little challenge I'll give you: What about going a tiny bit outside of your comfort zone and going a step further? I'll give an example of how I've gone outside of my comfort zone. Despite my love of bumble bees, I'm not a very good gardener. I don't like dirt or getting dirty. I wanted to help my local bumble bees. I did some reading on how to grow a garden, bought some flowers, and planted them in my backyard. I got a bit dirty and you know what? It wasn't so bad after all. Most of the flowers survived! And, one day, I saw bumble bees foraging on them. I think, with time and practice, I'll get better at my flower garden.

Each individual worker bee brings back to her colony only a bit of nectar and pollen. It's not enough to feed everyone. But with enough worker bees bringing back their own little bit of food, it all adds up and it does feed the colony. I think our small actions can be like that when it comes to helping wild bumble bees, or with any other environmental issue for that matter: If each of us does just a little bit, all these bits add up to becoming a lot.

So, big or small, what will your bit for the wild bumble bees be?

Glossary

Abdomen—The rear section of a bumble bee's body, the belly. It contains the digestive and reproductive organs and the stinger.

Acaricides—Chemicals used to treat ticks and mites, including **VAMPIRE MITES**. When eaten by bees, it reduces their ability to get rid of **TOXINS** in their body. This makes the bees sick.

Acute bee paralysis virus—A virus that **VAMPIRE MITES** can spread to adult honey bees. An infected adult bee trembles, is unable to fly, is increasingly paralyzed, and eventually dies.

Afterswarm—Once a **SWARM** of honey bees leaves a colony, if the colony is still crowded, a new queen may lead some worker bees in another swarm to look for a new place to make a nest.

Anther—The part of a flower that makes **POLLEN**. Bumble bees grab on to the anther and shake it during **BUZZ POLLINATION**.

Apiary (plural: apiaries)—Places where people keep honey bee hives.

Apicystis bombi—A **MICROSCOPIC**, one-celled, sausage-shaped **PARASITE** that lives in the **FAT BODY** of bumble bees and other insects. It tends to shrink the fat body in bumble bees.

Behavioral Ecology Tag (BEEtag)—A tiny square of waterproof, tear-resistant paper that scientists can glue onto the **THORAX** of a bee when they want to keep track of her movements. Each little square of paper has a unique arrangement of pixels on it, and a computer program can track the movement of the bee using her tag.

Bioaccumulation—When there is a buildup of a toxic substance over time in an animal.

Brood—All of the immature or baby bees in a colony.

Brood cells—Little wax compartments or "cells" that bees make where baby bees can grow.

Buzz pollination—A method used by bumble bees to collect **POLLEN** from certain flowers. Bumble bees grab the **ANTHERS** of the flower with their **MANDIBLES**, curl their body around the anthers, and vibrate their flight muscles really fast. This causes the pollen to fall onto their belly. Buzz pollination is also called sonication.

Citizen science—A project where non-scientist members of the public give their observations to the lead scientist(s). Their data may be used in the project.

Collapse—The disappearance, illness, or death of many or most worker bees, which means the colony has little or no chance to survive. It can also refer to the disappearance, illness, or death of a whole population of a bee **SPECIES**.

Colony collapse disorder (CCD)—A mysterious occurrence in which most or all of the adult honey bees in a hive disappear, with no trace of dead bees. The **BROOD**, the **POLLEN** and honey stores, and the queen bee are left behind. Sometimes a small cluster of worker bees is also left. Honey bee colonies afflicted with CCD are pretty much doomed.

Commercial honey bee keepers—People who rent their numerous honey bee hives to farmers so the bees can pollinate their crops. Often these beekeepers also sell their bees' honey.

Compound eyes—The large eyes of insects, made up of thousands of individual hexagon-shaped lenses called **FACETS**, which allow the insect to see.

Corbicula (plural: corbiculae)—The smooth and slightly spoon-shaped section on the back legs of **POLLEN**-collecting bees. The bee stores pollen here in clumps in order to bring it back to the colony. It's also called the **POLLEN BASKET**.

Coumaphos—A product used by honey bee keepers to control **VAMPIRE MITES**.

Crithidia bombi—A **MICROSCOPIC**, one-celled **PARASITE** that lives in the intestines of bumble bees. It looks like a deflated balloon on a stick! It spreads when bumble bees come into contact with contaminated nest material or if they drink from flowers with contaminated **NECTAR**. It is often found in buff-tailed bumble bees.

Crop—The stomach of a bee where the **NECTAR** goes when the bee drinks from flowers. It is also called the **HONEY STOMACH**.

Decline—The shrinking of the number of bees (or other animals) found on the planet.

Deformed wing virus—A virus that **VAMPIRE MITES** can spread to adult honey bees. It causes honey bees to develop stubby, useless wings. Bees with this virus do not live long and are often kicked out of the hive.

Diazinon—A type of **INSECTICIDE** that was sprayed on crops. At one time it was also used to kill household insects.

DNA testing—Similar to how each person has their own unique fingerprint, each bumble bee **SPECIES** has its own pattern of DNA (deoxyribonucleic acid). DNA is found in cells, and it is like a **MICROSCOPIC** bead on a string that contains the instructions or recipe for how to build a living thing. To do a DNA test for a bumble bee, scientists take a tiny piece of a bumble bee's **TARSUS** (foot) and use special equipment to look at the DNA pattern. This is also called genetic testing.

Doorstep foragers—Animals that do not travel far from their home to collect food.

Drones—Male bees.

Ecosystem—The way in which the various plants and animals found in an area interact with each other.

Entomology—The scientific study of insects.

Ergosterol inhibiting fungicides (EI fungicides)—A chemical used to get rid of **FUNGUS**. When eaten by a bee, it reduces its ability to get rid of **TOXINS** in its body, making the bee sick.

Exoskeleton—A hard shell that covers the body of an insect.

Extinction—When a **SPECIES** dies out and no longer exists.

Facets—The tiny lenses that make up the **COMPOUND EYES** of insects.

Fat body—A loose tissue found inside an insect that stores food molecules. Queen bumble bees rely on energy stored in their fat bodies to provide them energy during

HIBERNATION. Fat bodies also help insects use food energy efficiently and help fight disease.

Feces—Poop.

Fipronil—A **PESTICIDE** that targets the insect brain and nervous system. Besides being used to treat crops, it is also found in a number of tick- and flea-control products for pets, as well as in some cockroach and ant traps. Fipronil weakens a bee's immune system, making it unable to fight off the effects of any viruses it might be exposed to.

Forage—To look for and gather food.

Fragmented—A word used to describe **HABITAT LOSS**. It happens when humans change the landscape, such as building roads and cities, so that what was once undisturbed land is now broken up into smaller pockets of land.

Fungicide—Something used to destroy a **FUNGUS** or **FUNGI**. Fungicides can be chemicals or biological organisms.

Fungus (plural: fungi)—A kingdom of living organisms that are separate from animals and plants. They spread spores, which are similar to seeds, to allow them to reproduce, but are usually too small to see. Fungi include mushrooms, yeasts, and molds, and many fungi can only be seen with a microscope. Some types of fungi are harmful to bumble bees.

Ganglia—Nerve centers (clusters of **NEURONS**) in the bee's body that control different body parts.

Genetic variety—Individual differences in offspring caused by differences in DNA passed from parent to offspring. These differences can help the offspring better adapt to stress and disease.

Genetics—A branch of biology focused on how organisms inherit traits from their parents. It's all about **DNA** (deoxyribonucleic acid) and genes, variety, and heredity.

Habitat loss—The shrinking in size of the natural area in which an animal lives, usually because of human activity.

Handling time—The amount of time a bee takes to get food from a flower.

Hemolymph—Bee blood.

Hibernation—When animals hide and stay in a sleeplike state during the winter months.

Honey stomach—The stomach of a bee where the **NECTAR** goes when it drinks from flowers. It is also called the **CROP**.

Imidacloprid (IM)—One of the most widely used **PESTICIDES** that is toxic to bees. It is in the **NEONICOTINOID** group, sold under the names Confidor, Admire, and Gaucho.

Inbreeding—When males of a **SPECIES** start breeding with females that are closely related to them. This will cause new generations to have less **GENETIC VARIETY**, which can cause them to be less able to ward off stress and infections.

Insect growth regulator—A type of **PESTICIDE** that is sprayed on adult insects, and these adults carry the pesticide back to their nests where it kills eggs, **LARVAE**, and pupae.

Insecticides—Chemicals that kill insects.

Invasive—Referring to a new plant or animal that is introduced to an area. It has no predators to control its population. It spreads quickly and widely, and is harmful to the **NATIVE SPECIES** of an area.

Invertebrates—Animals that don't have a backbone or spine.

Israeli paralysis virus—A virus that **VAMPIRE MITES** can spread to honey bees. It can infect developing bees as well as adult bees. An adult infected bee trembles, is unable to fly, is increasingly paralyzed, and eventually dies.

Kashmir bee virus—A virus that **VAMPIRE MITES** can spread to honey bees. Adult honey bees die within a few days of being exposed to the virus.

Labial gland—A gland inside a male bumble bee's head that makes a **PHEROMONE** to attract queen bumble bees. The male bee "paints" the pheromone on objects with his bushy mustache.

Larva (plural: larvae)—A baby bee that looks like a little white worm. Larvae hatch from the eggs laid by the queen bee, transform into a pupa, and then grow into an adult bee.

LD$_{50}$—The amount of **PESTICIDE** that can kill 50 percent (half) of a sample of honey bees. (LD stands for *lethal dose*.)

Mandibles—A bumble bee's pincerlike mouthparts.

Mental representations—Pictures you create in your mind.

Microscopic—Too small to see with your eyes alone. You need a microscope to see it.

Mite—A tiny arachnid that infests bee colonies and other animals and plants. Mites often spread disease or weaken an animal or plant.

Monocultures—The growth of only one type of crop in a large field.

Native—An animal or plant that is naturally found in an area.

Nectar—The sugary liquid flowers make that bumble bees drink for energy.

Nectar robbing—When bumble bees chew holes in the base of tube-shaped flowers and suck the flower's **NECTAR** out through these holes. The bees that first chew the holes are called primary nectar robbers, and bees that reuse the holes are called secondary nectar robbers.

Nematode—A very tiny worm that lives as a **PARASITE** in animals and plants. Nematodes also live freely in soil or water.

Neonicotinoid (neonics)—A group of chemicals used to protect crops from insect pests. They have a similar chemical structure to nicotine, the addictive drug found in tobacco. They are very toxic to bees: They attach to specific parts of their brain, can cause the bee to become paralyzed, and can eventually cause death.

Neuron—A brain cell.

Niche overlap—When two or more **SPECIES** of plants or animals share the same food, living space, predators, and other things in their day-to-day living. For example, if a new species of bumble bee is introduced in an area, they might have a niche overlap with wild bumble bees that naturally live there, because they have to compete for flowers and nest sites.

Nosema bombi—A **MICROSCOPIC**, one-celled **FUNGUS**-type **PARASITE** that invades the intestines of bumble bees.

Nosema ceranae—A single-celled **PARASITE** that invades honey bees' guts and gives them diarrhea. It makes the bee weak and unable to absorb nutrients from food. It is believed to be partly responsible for CCD.

Ocelli—The three small eyes found between the **COMPOUND EYES** of a bee. The ocelli are used to detect light intensity and perhaps help the bee know how its body is positioned in relation to the space around it; they cannot focus or make images.

Paper wasps—Large, flying, stinging insects. They make their nests by gathering fibers from dead wood and plant stems and mixing it with their saliva. The result is a gray or brown papery structure. Like bumble bees, paper wasps live in colonies with a queen and workers.

Parasite—A creature that lives on or inside an animal, feeding off that animal and causing it harm.

Pathogen—A microorganism that can cause disease. Viruses and fungi are examples of pathogens.

Pathogen spillover—When an organism that causes disease spreads from an infected group to a healthy group. For example, when heavily infected commercial bumble bees spread **PATHOGENS** to wild bumble bees.

Pathology—The study of diseases: where they come from, how they develop, what they do to living things, and how we can get rid of them.

Pesticide—Something that destroys pests such as weeds, insects, or fungi. Usually they are human-made chemicals applied to crops, lawns, or gardens. Pesticides that target weeds or plants are called herbicides. Pesticides that target insects are called **INSECTICIDES**, and pesticides that target fungi care called **FUNGICIDES**.

Pheromone—A chemical signal produced by animals to alert individuals of the same **SPECIES**.

Pigment—Color. Specifically, it is a substance in an animal or plant's cells that gives it color.

Pollen—The powdery stuff that flowers make. It is commonly yellow but can be a variety of colors. Bumble bees collect pollen and feed it to baby bees as a source of **PROTEIN**.

Pollen basket—The smooth and slightly spoon-shaped section on the back legs of **POLLEN**-collecting bees. The bee stores pollen here in clumps in order to bring it back to the colony. It's also called the **CORBICULA** (**plural: CORBICULAE**).

Pollinator—An animal that moves **POLLEN** from the **ANTHER** of one flower to the **STIGMA** of another, allowing the plant to reproduce. Bumble bees are pollinators, along with other bees (such as honey bees), butterflies, moths, beetles, flies, bats, and certain **SPECIES** of birds.

Pollinator biocontrol vector technology—The use of bumble bees (or other **POLLINATORS**) to deliver plant treatments.

Predatory mite—Tiny creatures related to spiders and ticks that attack and feed on spider mites, which are considered a pest. Predatory mites have been bred and sold as a way to control spider mites in food crops.

Proboscis—A bumble bee's long tongue that is used to suck up **NECTAR** from flowers.

Protein—A nutrient found in **POLLEN** that baby bees need to eat in order to grow into adult bees. Queen honey bees also need protein to start laying eggs.

Pyrethroids—A class of **PESTICIDES** that are also found in many commercial household **INSECTICIDES**.

Queen excluders—Entrance holes in commercial bumble bee colonies that are too small for queens to fit through and escape into the wild.

Radio-frequency identification tag (RFID tag)—Small tags that look like tiny computer chips, that are glued to a bumble bee's **THORAX**. When a bumble bee with an RFID tag runs or flies past an RFID reader, it is like scanning an item at the grocery store: The unique number from the bumble bee's tag is recorded by a computer. RFID tags are used by scientists when they want to keep track of the movement of individual bees.

Range—The area throughout which a **SPECIES** of plant or animal can be found.

Royal jelly—A thick white liquid that worker honey bees make from glands near their **MANDIBLES**. They feed this to the queen bee, and it provides her with the **PROTEIN** she needs to start laying eggs.

Scat—Poop.

Shipping fever—When the stress from traveling lowers an animal's resistance to **PARASITES** and disease.

Social bees—**SPECIES** of bees that live in a colony. Social bees work together to raise baby bees, keep the nest clean, and generally help the colony to survive.

Social learning—When an animal learns from another animal by watching them.

Solitary bees—**SPECIES** of bees that do not live in a colony. Instead, they live by themselves and leave their eggs to develop on their own.

Species—A group of animals or plants with similar features (for example, fur color pattern) that can breed with each other. There are over 250 species of bumble bees.

Specimen—An individual member of a **SPECIES** that is studied by scientists. It represents all members of its species.

Spiracles—Holes found along the side of an insect's body that they use to breathe through.

Sterile—When an animal is not able to produce offspring.

Stigma—The sticky part of a flower that receives **POLLEN**.

Subjective experience—The quality of something (such as an emotion) that happens inside of us.

Sublethal effects—An effect that does not kill a plant or animal but can still harm it. For example, one potential sublethal effect of **PESTICIDES** is to make it harder for bees to learn which flowers they can collect **POLLEN** and **NECTAR** from.

Swarm—The term for when a honey bee colony becomes too crowded, and the original queen and about half of the worker bees fly out of the nest in a swirling mass. They often cluster on a tree branch, waiting while some bees go off to search for somewhere to start a new home.

Synapse—The connection between brain cells (**NEURONS**).

Systemic pesticides—A chemical that protects a plant, where it is taken up by the roots of the plant, enters the sap, and travels to the plant's stem, leaves, flowers, and **POLLEN**.

Tarsus (plural: tarsi)—An insect's "foot," or the last section of their leg farthest from their body.

Thermoregulation—The ability to keep a steady temperature. With bumble bees, this often means the ability of the colony to keep a steady nest temperature.

Thorax—The middle section of an insect's body, behind the head, where the legs and wings are attached.

Torpor—A kind of deep-sleep state when bees stop moving. It happens when a bee becomes too cold or when she is hibernating.

Toxins—Poisons that harm the bodies of living things.

Trachea—Breathing tubes inside the insect, attached to the **SPIRACLES**, which deliver air to the insect's cells.

Tracheal mites—Very tiny creatures that live in the **TRACHEA** of bumble bees. They make bumble bees sick and too tired to **FORAGE**.

Transect—The path or route someone takes when they are counting and recording the number of times they see a **SPECIES**.

Vampire mite or varroa mite (*Varroa destructor*)—Tiny, reddish-colored, disc-shaped **PARASITES** that latch onto honey bees and suck out their blood. They weaken the honey bee immune system and give viruses to the bees.

Vector—A word in biology used to refer to a living thing that transmits or carries something such as a **FUNGUS**, bacterium, or virus.

References

BOOKS

Costa, James T. *Darwin's Backyard: How Small Experiments Led to a Big Theory.* New York: W. W. Norton & Company, 2017.

Darwin, Charles. *On the Effects of Cross and Self-Fertilisation in the Vegetable Kingdom.* London: John Murray, 1876.

Gould, James L., and Carol Grant Gould. *The Honey Bee.* New York: Scientific American Library, 1988.

Goulson, Dave. *Bee Quest: In Search of Rare Bees.* London: Jonathan Cape, 2017.

———. *Bumblebees: Behaviour, Ecology, and Conservation.* 2nd ed. New York: Oxford University Press, 2010.

———. *A Sting in the Tale: My Adventures with Bumblebees.* London: Vintage Books, 2013.

Schacker, Michael. *A Spring without Bees: How Colony Collapse Disorder Has Endangered Our Food Supply.* Guilford, CT: The Lyons Press, 2008.

Sladen, Frederick William Lambert. *The Humble-Bee: Its Life-History and How to Domesticate It, With Descriptions of All the British Species of* Bombus *and* Psithyrus. London: MacMillan and Co., 1912.

Williams, Paul H., Robbin W. Thorp, Leif L. Richardson, and Sheila R. Colla. *Bumble Bees of North America: An Identification Guide.* Princeton, NJ: Princeton University Press, 2014.

Wilson-Rich, Noah, Kelly Allin, Norman Carreck, and Andrea Quigley. *The Bee: A Natural History.* Princeton, NJ: Princeton University Press, 2014.

Winston, Mark L. *The Biology of the Honey Bee.* Cambridge, MA: Harvard University Press, 1987.

BOOK CHAPTERS

Bonmatin, J. M., I. Moineau, R. Charvet, M. E. Colin, C. Fleche, and E. R. Bengsch. "Behaviour of Imidacloprid in Fields. Toxicity for Honey Bees." In Lichtfouse, Eric, Jan Schwarzbauer, and Didier Robert, Eds. *Environmental Chemistry: Green Chemistry and Pollutants in Ecosystems,* 483–94. New York: Springer, 2005.

Kevan, Peter G., Jean-Pierre Kapongo, Mohammad Al-mazra'awi, and Les Shipp. "Honey Bees, Bumble Bees, and Biocontrol: New Alliances Between Old Friends." In James, Rosalind R., and Theresa L. Pitts-Singer, Eds. *Bee Pollination in Agricultural Ecosystems,* 65–79. London: Oxford University Press, 2008.

MAGAZINE ARTICLES

Batra, Suzanne W. T. "Solitary Bees." *Scientific American* 250, no. 2 (1984): 120–127.

Chittka, Lars, and Catherine Wilson. "Bee-Brained." *Aeon* magazine, 2018. Retrieved December 1, 2018, from https://aeon.co/essays/inside-the-mind-of-a -bee-is-a-hive-of-sensory-activity.

———. "The Secret Inner Life of the Bumblebee." *Fast Company,* December 27, 2018. Retrieved March 17, 2019, from https://www.fastcompany.com /90286397/the-secret-inner-life-of-the-bumblebee.

Goulson, Dave. "Argentinian Invasion!" *Buzzword* no. 21 (2013): 17–18.

"How the Bumble Bee Got Its Stripes." *EurekAlert!,* Retrieved April 29, 2019, from https://www.eurekalert.org/pub_releases/2019-04/ps-htb042919.php.

Sijmonsma, Arlette. "How the Bumble Bee Coincidentally Saved the Greenhouse Industry." *Hortidaily,* 2017. Retrieved April 27, 2019, from https://www .hortidaily.com/article/35851/How-the-bumble bee-coincidentally-saved-the -greenhouse-industry/.

WEBSITES

Biobest. (n.d.). "Masculino-System (B.t.)." Retrieved April 28, 2019, from http:// www.biobestgroup.com/en/biobest/products/bumblebee-pollination-4460 /bumblebee-hives-6329/masculino-system-%28b-t-%29-4626/.

Biobest. (n.d.). "Reaching Out to Growers: Biobest as a Global Player." Retrieved April 28, 2019, from http://www.biobestgroup.com/en/biobest/about-us /reaching-out-to-growers%3A-biobest-as-a-global-player-15372/.

275

British Columbia Ministry of Agriculture. "Pesticide toxicity and hazard."
April 2017. Retrieved February 3, 2019, from https://www2.gov.bc.ca/assets
/gov/farming-natural-resources-and-industry/agriculture-and-seafood/animal
-and-crops/plant-health/pesticide-toxicity-hazard.pdf.

Bumblebee.org. "Bumblebee Tongue and Mouthparts. " 2016. Retrieved May 21,
2018, from www.bumblebee.org/bodyTongue.htm.

Bumblebee Conservation Trust. "Commercial Bumblebees Policy." 2016. Retrieved
April 8, 2019, from: https://www.bumblebeeconservation.org/images/uploads
/Policies/Commercial_bumblebees_policy.pdf.

Bumblebee Conservation Trust. "Why Are Bumblebees Such Good Pollinators?"
2016. Retrieved July 16, 2019, from https://bumblebeeconservation.org/about
-bees/faqs/buzz-pollination/. Content no longer available.

———. "Heath bumblebee (*Bombus jonellus*)." 2018. Retrieved November 18, 2018,
from: https://www.bumblebeeconservation.org/white-tailed-bumblebees
/heath-bumblebee/.

———. "Introducing the Tree bumblebee (*Bombus hypnorum*)." 2018. Retrieved
November 18, 2018, from https://www.bumblebeeconservation.org/tree
-bumblebee-bombus-hypnorum/.

———. "Ruderal bumblebee (*Bombus ruderatus*)." 2018. Retrieved November 18,
2018, from https://www.bumblebeeconservation.org/white-tailed-bumblebees
/ruderal-bumblebee/.

———. "White-tailed bumblebee (*Bombus lucorum*)." 2018. Retrieved
November 18, 2018, from https://www.bumblebeeconservation.org/white
-tailed-bumblebees/white-tailed-bumblebee/.

Canadian Broadcasting Corporation (CBC). "Canada Bans Neonic Pesticides
Implicated in Bee Declines." August 17, 2018. Retrieved February 17, 2019,
from https://www.cbc.ca/radio/quirks/august-18-2018-canada-bans-neonics
-tracking-animals-from-space-and-more-1.4786729/canada-bans-neonic
-pesticides-implicated-in-bee-declines-1.4786738.

Cox, Darryl. "Bumblebees of the World . . . #1 Bombus dahlbomii." Bumblebee
Conservation Trust, 2019. Retrieved April 7, 2019, from https://www
.bumblebeeconservation.org/bumblebees-of-the-world-1-bombus
-dahlbomii/.

European Commission. "Neonicotinoids." 2018. Retrieved February 17, 2019, from https://ec.europa.eu/food/plant/pesticides/approval_active_substances /approval_renewal/neonicotinoids_en.

Food and Agriculture Organization of the United Nations. "Pollinators Vital to Our Food Supply Under Threat." February 26, 2016. Retrieved October 8, 2018, from http://www.fao.org/news/story/en/item/384726/icode/.

Garvey, Kathy Keatley. "Dr. Robbin Thorp: 1933–2019." *Entomology & Nematology News*, 2019. Retrieved June 8, 2019, from https://ucanr.edu/blogs /blogcore/postdetail.cfm?postnum=30459.

Government of Canada. "Species Profile: Rusty-patched Bumble Bee." 2011. Retrieved May 26, 2019, from https://wildlife-species.canada.ca/species-risk -registry/species/speciesDetails_e.cfm?sid=1081.

Government of Newfoundland and Labrador. "Wild Life Regulations Under the Wild Life Act, Part VI, Section 83." 2018. Retrieved March 4, 2019, from https://www.assembly.nl.ca/legislation/sr/regulations/rc961156.htm#83_.

Hatfield, R., S. Jepsen, R. Thorp, L. Richardson, and S. Colla. "*Bombus terricola*. The IUCN Red List of Threatened Species 2015: e.T44937505A46440206." 2015. http://dx.doi.org/10.2305/IUCN.UK.2015-2.RLTS .T44937505A46440206.en. Downloaded on May 26, 2019.

Hatfield, R., S. Jepsen, R. Thorp, L. Richardson, S. Colla, Jordan S. Foltz, and E. Evans. "*Bombus affinis*. The IUCN Red List of Threatened Species 2015: e.T44937399A46440196." 2015. http://dx.doi.org/10.2305/IUCN.UK.2015 -2.RLTS.T44937399A46440196.en. Downloaded on May 26, 2019.

Hatfield, R., S. Jepsen, R. Thorp, L. Richardson, S. Colla. and Jordan S. Foltz. "*Bombus occidentalis*. The IUCN Red List of Threatened Species 2015: e.T44937492A46440201." 2015. http://dx.doi.org/10.2305/IUCN.UK.2015 -2.RLTS.T44937492A46440201.en. Downloaded on January 26, 2019.

International Union for Conservation of Nature (IUCN). (2019). "Commercial Bumble Bee Policy Statement." Retrieved April 8, 2019, from https://www.iucn.org/ssc -groups/invertebrates/bumblebee-specialist-group/commercial-bumblebee-policy -statement.

IUCN Red List. "How the Red List is Used," 2019. Retrieved May 26, 2019, from https://www.iucnredlist.org/about/uses.

Koppert Biological Systems. (n.d.). "Our history: Jan Koppert, Founder of Koppert Biological Systems in 1967." Retrieved January 14, 2020, from https://www.koppert.com/about-koppert/our-company/.

———. "Koppert Locations and Suppliers." 2019. Retrieved April 28, 2019, from https://www.koppert.com/about-koppert/koppert-locations-and-suppliers/.

Merriam-Webster online. "Bioaccumulation" [Def. 1]. (n.d.). Retrieved June 12, 2019, from https://www.merriam-webster.com/dictionary/bioaccumulation.

———. "Genetics" [Def. 1]. (n.d.). Retrieved June 5, 2019, from https://www.merriam-webster.com/dictionary/genetics.

Morales, C., J. Montalva, M. Arbetman, M.A. Aizen, C. Smith-Ramírez, L. Vieli, and R. Hatfield. "*Bombus dahlbomii*. The IUCN Red List of Threatened Species 2016: e.T21215142A100240441." 2016. http://dx.doi.org/10.2305/IUCN.UK.2016-3.RLTS.T21215142A100240441.en. Downloaded on January 26, 2019.

Newfoundland and Labrador Beekeeping Association. "Import Ban on Bumble Bees," 2015. Retrieved March 4, 2019, from http://www.nlbeekeeping.ca/issues-advocacy/importation-restrictions/#_edn2.

Salvemos Nuestro Abejorro (Save Our Bumble Bee). (n.d.) "Quienes Somos (Who We Are)." Retrieved June 10, 2019, from https://salvemosnuestroabejorro.wordpress.com/about/.

Sutter, John D. "The Old Man and the Bee." CNN, December 13, 2016. Retrieved May 20, 2019, from https://www.cnn.com/2016/12/11/us/vanishing-sutter-franklins-bumblebee/index.html.

The Measure of Things. (n.d.). "How Heavy Is 500 Tonnes?" Retrieved April 11, 2019, from https://www.bluebulbprojects.com/measureofthings/results.php?comp=weight&unit=tnsm&amt=500&sort=pr&p=2.

The White House, Office of the Press Secretary. "Fact sheet: The Economic Challenge Posed by Declining Pollinator Populations." June 20, 2014. Retrieved October 8, 2018, from https://obamawhitehouse.archives.gov/the-press-office/2014/06/20/fact-sheet-economic-challenge-posed-declining-pollinator-populations.

Tourism Australia. "Facts and Planning: Weather in Australia." 2019. Retrieved March 28, 2019, from https://www.australia.com/en/facts-and-planning/weather-in-australia.html.

United States Department of Agriculture. "Bee Research Laboratory: Beltsville, Maryland." Retrieved January 8, 2019, from https://www.ars.usda.gov /northeast-area/beltsville-md-barc/beltsville-agricultural-research-center/bee -research-laboratory/.

University of Minnesota Extension. "Minnesota Bee Atlas: Bumble Bee Survey." 2019. Retrieved May 11, 2019, from https://apps.extension.umn.edu /environment/citizen-science/bee-atlas/bumble-bees/.

University of Minnesota Extension Citizen Science. "Citizen Science in the Classroom: Pollinators." September 6, 2017. Retrieved May 11, 2019, from https://www.youtube.com/watch?v=6LCFP2eqPPc.

US Fish & Wildlife Service. ECOS Environmental Conservation Online System. "Rusty-patched Bumble Bee (*Bombus affinis*)." 2017. Retrieved May 26, 2019, from https://ecos.fws.gov/ecp0/profile/speciesProfile;jsessionid=8B6AD0C8 C7A3267C847265B2E34F3B32?spcode=I0WI.

Encyclopedia Britannica Online, s. v. "Fabaceae," accessed April 1, 2020, https:// www.britannica.com/plant/Fabaceae.

Encyclopedia Britannica Online, s. v. "Hectare," accessed April 1, 2020, https:// www.britannica.com/science/hectare.

Wildlife Preservation Canada. "A Flower Patch for the Rusty-patched." 2019. Retrieved May 12, 2019, from https://wildlifepreservation.ca/a-flower-patch -for-the-rusty-patched/.

INTERVIEWS

Colla, Sheila R., April 30, 2019. Personal interview.

Hatfield, Richard, June 6, 2019. Personal interview.

Hicks, Barry, March 4, 2019. Personal interview.

Jepsen, Sarina, May 13, 2019. Personal interview.

Morales, Carolina L., November 26, 2018. Personal interview.

Rowe, Genevieve, May 21, 2019. Personal interview.

Toth, Amy, April 15, 2019. Personal interview.

VIDEOS AND PRESENTATIONS

Tompkins, Hayley. Hayley Tompkins (MSc, Environmental Science), University of Guelph 3MT Finalist, presenting "Building the Buzz: Artificial Nest Boxes as a Conservation and Monitoring Tool for Bumble Bees." April 5, 2019. Retrieved May 11, 2019, from https://www.youtube.com/watch?v=kUUSc-9bZc8&app =desktop.

Tompkins, Hayley, and Genevieve Rowe. "The Buzz about Bumble Bees." March 2019. Workshop presented at Wilfrid Laurier University, Waterloo, ON, Canada.

REPORTS

Comont, Richard, & Stephanie Miles. *BeeWalk Annual Report 2019*. Bumblebee Conservation Trust, Stirling, Scotland, UK, 2019.

Gurian-Sherman, D. *Alternatives to Neonicotinoid Insecticide-Coated Corn Seed: Agroecological Methods are Better for Farmers and the Environment.* Center for Food Safety, 2017. Retrieved February 23, 2019, from https://www.center forfoodsafety.org/reports/4954/alternatives-to-neonicotinoid-insecticide-coated -corn-seed-agroecological-methods-are-better-for-farmers-and-the-environment.

Jenkins, Peter T. *Net Loss—Economic Efficacy and Costs of Neonicotinoid Insecticides Used as Seed Coatings: Updates from the United States and Europe.* Center for Food Safety, 2016. Retrieved February 21, 2019, from https://www.centerforfoodsafety .org/reports/4591/net-losseconomic-efficacy-and-costs-of-neonicotinoid -insecticides-used-as-seed-coatings-updates-from-the-united-states-and-europe.

Jepsen, Sarina, Elaine Evans, Robbin Thorp, Richard Hatfield, and Scott Hoffman Black. *Petition to List the Rusty-patched Bumble Bee* Bombus affinis *(Cresson), 1863 as an Endangered Species Under the U.S. Endangered Species Act.* 2013. Retrieved May 25, 2019, from https://xerces.org/publications/petitions -comments/petition-to-list-rusty-patched-bumble-bee-bombus-affinis-cresson.

Johnson, Renée. *Honey Bee Colony Collapse Disorder: CRS report for Congress.* Congressional Research Service, 2010.

Stevens, Sarah, & Peter Jenkins. *Heavy Costs: Weighing the Value of Neonicotinoid Insecticides in Agriculture.* Center for Food Safety, 2014. Retrieved February 19, 2019, from https://www.centerforfoodsafety.org/reports/2999 /heavy-costs-weighing-the-value-of-neonicotinoid-insecticides-in-agriculture.

The Xerces Society for Invertebrate Conservation, Defenders of Wildlife, & Center for Food Safety. *A Petition to the State of California Fish and Game Commission to List the Crotch Bumble Bee* (Bombus crotchii), *Franklin's Bumble Bee* (Bombus franklini), *Suckley Cuckoo Bumble Bee* (Bombus suckleyi), *and Western Bumble Bee* (Bombus occidentalis occidentalis) *as endangered under the California Endangered Species Act.* 2018. Retrieved May 22, 2019, from https://xerces.org/publications/policy-statements /california-esa-bumble-bee-petition-2018.

Thorp, Robbin, Sarina Jepsen, Sarah Foltz Jordan, Elaine Evans, and Scott Hoffman Black. *Petition to List Franklin's Bumble Bee* Bombus franklini (*Frison*), *1921 as an Endangered Species under the U.S. Endangered Species Act.* 2010. Retrieved May 22, 2019, from https://xerces.org/publications/policy -statements/petition-to-list-franklins-bumble-bee-under-esa-2010.

SCIENTIFIC JOURNAL ARTICLES

Adamo, Shelley Anne. "Do Insects Feel Pain? A Question at the Intersection of Animal Behaviour, Philosophy and Robotics." *Animal Behaviour* 118 (August 2016): 75–79. DOI: 10.1016/j.anbehav.2016.05.005.

Aizen, Marcelo A., Carolina L. Morales, and Juan M. Morales. "Invasive Mutualists Erode Native Pollination Webs." *PLoS Biology* 6, no. 2 (February 2008): e31. DOI: 10.1371/journal.pbio.0060031. Dataset S1. The Ten Pollination Networks: https://doi.org/10.1371/journal.pbio.0060031.sd001.

Alem, Sylvain, Clint J. Perry, Xingfu Zhu, Olli J. Loukola, Thomas Ingraham, Eirik Søvik, and Lars Chittka. "Associative Mechanisms Allow for Social Learning and Cultural Transmission of String Pulling in an Insect." *PLoS Biology* 14, no.10, e1002564 (2016). DOI: 10.1371/journal.pbio1002564.

Arbetman, Marina P., Ivan Meeus, Carolina L. Morales, Marcelo A. Aizen, and Guy Smagghe. "Alien Parasite Hitchhikes to Patagonia on Invasive Bumblebee." *Biological Invasions* 15 (2013): 489–494.

Arce, Andres N., Ana Ramos Rodrigues, Jiajun Yu, Thomas J. Colgan, Yannick Wurm, and Richard J. Gill. "Foraging Bumble Bees acquire a Preference for Neonicotinoid-Treated Food with Prolonged Exposure." *Proceedings of the Royal Society* B (2018): 285. 20180655. DOI: 10.1098/rspb.2018.0655.

Arrese, Estela L., and Jose L. Soulages. "Insect Fat Body: Energy, Metabolism, and Regulation." *Annual Review of Entomology* 55 (2010): 207–225.

Arretz, P. V., and R. P. Macfarlane. "The Introduction of *Bombus ruderatus* to Chile for Red Clover Pollination." *Bee World* 67, no. 1 (1986): 15–22.

Baracchi, David, Mathieu Lihoreau, and Martin Giurfa. "Do Insects Have Emotions? Some Insights from Bumble Bees." *Frontiers in Behavioral Neuroscience* 11 (2017): 157. DOI: 10.3389/fnbeh.2017.00157.

Bishop, Christine A., Alison J. Moran, Michelle C. Toshack, Elizabeth Elle, France Maisonneuve, and Johne E. Elliott. "Hummingbirds and Bumble Bees Exposed to Neonicotinoid and Organophosphate Insecticides in the Fraser Valley, British Columbia, Canada." *Environmental Toxicology and Chemistry* 37, no.8 (2018): 2143–2152. DOI: 10.1002/etc.4174.

Buttermore, R. E. "Observations of Successful *Bombus terrestris* (L.) (Hymenoptera: Apidae) Colonies in Southern Tasmania." *Australian Journal of Entomology* 36 (1997): 251–254.

Cameron, Sydney A., Haw Chuan, Jeffrey D. Lozier, Michelle A. Duennes, and Robbin Thorp. "Test of the Invasive Pathogen Hypothesis of Bumble Bee Decline in North America." *Proceedings of the National Academy of Sciences* 113, no.16 (2016): 4386–4391. DOI: 10.1073/pnas.1525266113.

Cameron, Sydney A., Jeffery D. Lozier, James P. Strange, Jonathan B. Koch, Nils Cordes, Leellen F. Solter, and Terry L. Griswold. "Patterns of Widespread Decline in North American Bumble Bees." *Proceedings of the National Academy of Sciences,* 108, no. 2 (2011): 662–667. DOI: 10.1073/pnas.1014743108.

Chen, Yan Ping, Jeffery S. Pettis, Miguel Corona, Wei Ping Chen, Cong Jun Li, Marla Spivak, et al. "Israeli Acute Paralysis Virus: Epidemiology, Pathogenesis, and Implications for Honey Bee Health." *PLoS Pathology* 10, no. 7 (2014): e1004261. DOI: 10.1371/journal.ppat.1004261.

Chittka, Lars, & Jeremy Niven. "Are Bigger Brains Better?" *Current Biology* 19 (2009): R995-R1008. DOI: 10.1016/j.cub.2009.08.023.

Colla, Sheila R., Michael C. Otterstatter, Robert J. Gegear, and James D. Thomson. "Plight of the Bumble bee: Pathogen Spillover from Commercial to Wild Populations." *Biological Conservation* 129 (2006): 461–467. DOI: 10.1016/j. biocon.2005.11.013.

Colla, Sheila, and Laurence Packer. "Evidence for Decline in Eastern North American Bumblebees (Hymenoptera: Apidae), with Special Focus on *Bombus affinis* Cresson." *Biodiversity and Conservation* 17 (2008): 1379–1391. DOI: 10.1007/s10531-008-9340-5.

Crall, James D., Nick Gravis., Andrew M. Mountcastle, and Stacey A. Combes. "BEEtag: A Low-Cost, Image-Based Tracking System for the Study of Animal Behavior and Locomotion." *PLoS ONE* 10, no. 9 (2015): e0136487. DOI: 10.1371/journal.pone.0136487.

Crall, James D., Callin M. Switzer, Robert L. Oppenheimer, Ashleen N. Ford Versypt, Biswadip Dey, Andrea Brown, Mackay Eyster, Claire Guérin, Naomi E. Pierce, Stacey A. Combes, and Benjamin L. de Bivort. "Neonicotinoid Exposure Disrupts Bumble Bee Nest Behavior, Social Networks, and Thermoregulation." *Science* 362 (2018): 683–686. DOI: 10.1126/science.aat1598.

Dafni, Amots, Peter Kevan, Caroline L. Gross, and Koichi Goka. "*Bombus terrestris*, Pollinator, Invasive and Pest: An Assessment of Problems Associated with its Widespread Introductions for Commercial Purposes." *Appl. Entomol. Zool.* 45, no. 1 (2010): 101–113.

Darwin, Leonard. "Memories of Down House." *The Nineteenth Century* 106 (1929): 118–123. Retrieved November 25, 2018, from: http://darwin-online .org.uk/content/frameset?itemID=A224&viewtype=text&pageseq=1.

David, Arthur, Cristina Botías, Alaa Abdul-Sada, Elizabeth Nicholls, Ellen L. Rotheray, Elizabeth M. Hill, and Dave Goulson. "Widespread Contamination of Wildflower and Bee-Collected Pollen with Complex Mixtures of Neonicotinoids and Fungicides Commonly Applied to Crops." *Environment International* 88 (2016): *169–178*. DOI: 10.1016/j.envint.2015.12.011.

Dehon, Manuel, Denis Michez, André Nel, Michael S. Engel, and Thibaut De Meulemeester. (2014). "Wing Shape of Four New Bee Fossils (Hymenoptera: Anthophila) Provides Insights to Bee Evolution." *PLoS ONE* 9, no.10 (2014): e108865. DOI: 10.1371/journal.pone.0108865.

de Miranda, Joachim R., Guido Cordoni, and Giles E. Budge. "The Acute Bee Paralysis Virus-Kashmir Bee Virus-Israeli Acute Paralysis Virus Complex." *Journal of Invertebrate Pathology* 103 (2010): S30-s47. DOI: 10.1016/j.jip.2009.06.014.

Dornhaus, Anna, and Lars Chittka. "Food Alert in Bumble Bees (*Bombus terrestris*): Possible Mechanisms and Evolutionary Implications." *Behavioral Ecology and Sociobiology* 50 (2001): 570–576.

Dornhaus, Anna, A. Brockmann, and Lars Chittka. "Bumble bees alert to food with pheromone from tergal gland." *Journal of Comparative Physiology A* 189 (2003): 47–51.

Dornhaus, Anna, and Lars Chittka. "Information Flow and Regulation of Foraging Activity in Bumble Bees (*Bombus* spp.)." *Apidologie* 35 (2004): 183–192. DOI: 10.1051/apido:2004002.

———. "Bumble Bees (*Bombus terrestris*) Store Both Food and Information in Honeypots." *Behavioural Ecology* 16 (2005): 661–666.

Drachman, David A. "Do We Have Brain to Spare?" *Neurology* 64, no. 12 (2005): 2004–2005.

Feltham, Hannah, Kirsty Park, and Dave Goulson. "Field Realistic Doses of Pesticide Imidacloprid Reduce Bumble Bee Pollen Foraging Efficiency." *Ecotoxicology* 23 (2014): 317–323. DOI: 10.1007/s10646-014-1189-7.

Freeman, R. B. "Charles Darwin on the Routes of Male Humble Bees." *Bulletin of the British Museum (Natural History), Historical Series* 3, no. 6 (1968): 177–189. Retrieved November 25, 2018 from: http://test.darwin-online.org.uk/converted/published/1968_bees_F1581.html.

Gegear, Robert J., Michael C. Otterstatter, and James D. Thomson. "Does Parasitic Infection Impair the Ability of Bumble Bees to Learn Flower-Handling Techniques?" *Animal Behaviour* 70 (2005): 209–215.

Gill, Richard J., and Nigel E. Raine. "Chronic Impairment of Bumble Bee Natural Foraging Behaviour Induced by Sublethal Pesticide Exposure." *Functional Ecology* 28 (2014): 1459–1471. DOI: 10.1111/1365-2435.12292.

Gill, Richard J., Oscar Ramos-Rodriguez, and Nigel E. Raine. "Combined Pesticide Exposure Severely Affects Individual- and Colony-Level Traits in Bees." *Nature* 491 (2012): 105–109. DOI: 10.1038/nature11585.

Goka, Koichi, Kimiko Okabe, Masahiro Yoneda, and Satomi Niwa. "Bumble Bee Commercialization Will Cause Worldwide Migration of Parasitic Mites." *Molecular Ecology* 10 (2001): 2095–2099.

Goulson, Dave. "Effects of Introduced Bees on Native Ecosystems." *Annual Review of Ecology, Evolution, and Systematics* 34 (2003): 1–26.

———. "An Overview of the Environmental Risks Posed by Neonicotinoid Insecticides." *Journal of Applied Ecology* 50 (2013): 977–987. DOI: 10.1111/1365-2664.12111.

Goulson, Dave, and Mick E. Hanley. "Distribution and Forage Use of Exotic Bumblebees in South Island, New Zealand." *New Zealand Journal of Ecology* 28, no. 2 (2004): 225–232.

Goulson, Dave, and William O. H. Hughes, "Mitigating the Anthropogenic Spread of Bee Parasites to Protect Wild Pollinators." *Biological Conservation* 191 (2015): 10–19. http://dx.doi.org/10.1016/j.biocon.2015.06.023.

Goulson, Dave, G. C. Lye, and B. Darvill. "Decline and Conservation of Bumble Bees." *Annual Review of Entomology* 53 (2008): 191–208. DOI: 10.1146/annurev.ento.53.103106.093454.

Graystock, Peter, Kathryn Yates, Sophie E. Evison, Ben Darvill, Dave Goulson, and William O. H. Hughes. "The Trojan Hives: Pollinator Pathogens, Imported and Distributed in Bumble Bee Colonies." *Journal of Applied Ecology* 50 (2013): 1207–1215. DOI: 10.1111/1365-2664.12134.

Graystock, Peter, Ivan Meeus, Guy Smagghe, Dave Goulson, and William O. H. Hughes. "The effects of single and mixed infections of *Apicystis bombi* and deformed wing virus in *Bombus terrestris*." *Parasitology* 143 (2016): 358–365.

Gurr, L. "The Introduction of Bumble Bees into North Island, New Zealand." *New Zealand Journal of Agricultural Research* 15, no. 3 (1972): 635–638.

Hicks, Barry. "Observations of the Nest Structure of *Osmia inermis* (Hymenoptera: Megachilidae) from Newfoundland, Canada." *Journal of the Acadian Entomological Society* 5 (2009): 12–18.

———. "Pollination of Lowbush Blueberry (*Vaccinium angustifolium*) in Newfoundland by Native and Introduced Bees." *Journal of the Acadian Entomological Society* 7 (2011): 108–118.

Hicks, Barry, B. L. Pilgrim, E. Perry, and H. D. Marshall. "Observations of Native Bumble Bees Inside of Commercial Colonies of *Bombus impatiens* (Hymenoptera: Apidae) and the Potential for Pathogen Spillover." *The Canadian Entomologist* 150 (2018): 520–531.

Hicks, Barry, and Julie Sircom. "Pollination of Commercial Cranberry (*Vaccinium macrocarpon* Ait.) by Native and Introduced Managed Bees in Newfoundland." *Journal of the Acadian Entomological Society* 12 (2016): 22–30.

Hines, Heather M. "Historical Biogeography, Divergence Times, and Diversification Patterns of Bumble Bees (Hymenoptera: Apidae: *Bombus*)." *Systematic Biology* 57, no.1 (2008): 58–75.

Hladik, Michelle L., Anson R. Main, and Dave Goulson. "Environmental Risks and Challenges associated with Neonicotinoid Insecticides." *Environmental Science & Technology* 52 (2018): 3329–3335. DOI: 10.1021/acs.est.7b06388.

Inari, Naoki, Teruyoshi Nagamitsu, Tanaka Kenta, Koichi Goka, and Tsutom Hiura, "Spatial and Temporal Pattern of Introduced *Bombus terrestris* Abundance in Hokkaido, Japan, and Its Potential Impact on Native Bumble Bees." *Population Ecology* 47 (2005): 77–82. DOI: 10.1007/s10144-004-0205-9.

Inoue, Maki N., Jun Yokoyama, & Izumi Washitani. "Displacement of Japanese Native Bumble Bees by the Recently Introduced *Bombus terrestris* (L.) (Hymenoptera: Apidae)." *Journal of Insect Conservation* 12 (2008): 135–146. DOI: 10.1007/s10841-007-9071-z.

Jeschke, Peter, & Ralf Nauen. "Neonicotinoids: From Zero to Hero in Insecticide Chemistry." *Pest Management Science* 64 (2008): 1084–1098. DOI: 10.1002/ps.1631.

Jeschke, Peter, Ralf Nauen, Michael Schindler, and Alfred Elbert. (2011). "Overview of the Status and Global Strategy for Neonicotinoids." *Journal of Agricultural and Food Chemistry* 59 (2011): 2897–2908. DOI: 10.1021/jf101303g.

Johnson, Sarah A., Meagan M. Tompkins, Hayley Tompkins, and Sheila R. Colla, "Artificial Domicile Use by Bumble Bees (*Bombus*; Hymenoptera: Apidae) in Ontario, Canada." *Journal of Insect Science* 19, no. 1 (2019). DOI 10.1093/jisesa/iey139.

Kawaguchi, Lina G., Kazuharu Ohashi, and Yukihiko Toquenaga. "Contrasting Responses of Bumble Bees to Feeding Conspecifics on Their Familiar and Unfamiliar Flowers." *Proceedings of the Royal Society B: Biological Sciences* 274 (2007): 2661–2667. DOI: 10.1098/rspb.2007.0860.

Kenta, Tanaka., Naoki Inari, Teruyoshi Nagamitsu, Koichi Goka, and Tsutom Hiura. "Commercialized European Bumble Bee Can Cause Pollination Disturbance: An Experiment on Seven Native Plant Species in Japan." *Biological Conservation* 134 (2007): 298–309. DOI: 10.1016/j.biocon.2006.07.023.

Kessler, Sébastien C., Erin Jo Tiedeken, Kerry L. Simcock, Sophie Derveau, Jessica Mitchell, Samantha Softley, Amy Radcliffe, Jane C. Stout, and Geraldine Wright. "Bees Prefer Food Containing Neonicotinoid Pesticides." *Nature* 521 (2015): 74–76. DOI: 10.1038/nature14414.

Kirk, William D. J. "The Colours of Pollen Available to Honey Bees Through the Year." *Bee World* 95, no. 3 (2018): 74–77.

Kondo, Natsuko, Daisei Yamanaka, Yuya Kanbe, Yoko Kawate Kunitake, Masahiro Yoneda, Koji Tsuchida, and Koichi Goka, "Reproductive Disturbance of Japanese Bumble Bees by the Introduced European Bumble Bee *Bombus terrestris*." *Naturwissenschaften* 96 (2009): 467–475. DOI: 10.1007/s00114-008-0495-4.

Koski, Matthew, and Laura F. Galloway. "Geographic Variation in Pollen Color is Associated with Temperature Stress." *New Phytologist* 218 (2018): 370–379. DOI: 10.1111/nph.14961.

Lawson, David A., Lars Chittka, Heather M. Whitney, and Sean A. Rands. "Bumblebees Distinguish Floral Scent Patterns, and Can Transfer These to Corresponding Visual Patterns." *Proceedings of the Royal Society B* 285 (2018): 20180661. DOI: 10.1098/rspb.2018.0661.

Leadbeater, Ellouise, and Lars Chittka. "Social Transmission of Nectar-Robbing Behaviour in Bumble-bees." *Proceedings of the Royal Society B* 275 (2008): 1669–1674. DOI: 10.1098/rspb.2008.0270.

Leza, Mar, Kristal M. Watrous, Jade Bratu, and S. Hollis Woodard, "Effects of Neonicotinoid Insecticide Exposure and Monofloral Diet on Nest-Founding Bumblebee Queens." *Proceedings of the Royal Society B* 285 (2018): 20180761. DOI: 10.1098/rspb.2018.0761.

Looney, Chris, James P. Strange, Maggie Freeman, and David Jennings. "The Expanding Pacific Northwest Range of *Bombus impatiens* Cresson and its Establishment in Washington State." *Biological Invasions* (2019). DOI: 10.1007/s10530-019-01970-6.

Loukola, Ollie J., Clint J. Perry, Louie Coscos, and Lars Chittka. "Bumblebees Show Cognitive Flexibility by Improving on an Observed Complex Behavior." *Science* 355 (2017): 833–836. DOI: 10.1126/science.aag2360.

Lye, G. C., Olivier LePais, and Dave Goulson, "Reconstructing Demographic Events from Population Genetic Data: The Introduction of Bumble Bees to New Zealand." *Molecular Ecology* 20 (2011): 2888–2900.

Maxim, L., and J. P. van der Sluijs, "Expert Explanations of Honey Bee Losses in Areas of Extensive Agriculture in France: Gaucho Compared with Other Supposed Causal Factors." *Environmental Research Letters* 5 (2010): 014006. DOI: 10.1088/1748-9326/5/1/014006.

Mitchell, E. A. D., B. Mulhauser, M. Mulot, A. Mutabazi, G. Glauser, and A. Aebi. "A Worldwide Survey of Neonicotinoids in Honey." *Science* 358 (2017): 109–111. DOI: 10.1126/science.aan3684.

Mommaerts, Veerle, Kurt Put, and Guy Smagghe. "*Bombus terrestris* as Pollinator-and-Vector to Suppress *Botrytis cinerea* in Greenhouse Strawberry." *Pest Management Science* 67 (2011): 1069–1075.

Morales, Carolina L., Marina P. Arbetman, Sydney A. Cameron, and Marcelo A. Aizen. "Rapid Ecological Replacement of a Native Bumble Bee by Invasive Species." *Frontiers in Ecology and the Environment* 11, no.10 (2013): 529–534.

Mullin, Christopher A., Maryann Frazier, James L. Frazier, Sara Ashcraft, Roger Simonds, Dennis vanEngelsdorp, and Jeffery S. Pettis. "High Levels of Miticides and Agrochemicals in North American Apiaries: Implications for Honey Bee Health." *PLoS ONE* 5, no. 3 (2010): e9754. DOI: 10.1371/journal.pone.0009754.

"Obituary: F. W. L. Sladen." *The Canadian Entomologist* 53, no.10 (1922): 240.

O'Connor, Steph, Kirsty J. Park, and Dave Goulson, D. "Humans Versus Dogs; a Comparison of Methods for the Detection of Bumble Bee Nests." *Journal of Apicultural Research* 51, no. 2 (2012): 204–211.

Oldroyd, Benjamin P. "What's Killing American Honey Bees?" *PLoS Biology* 5, no. 6 (2007): e168. DOI: 10.1371/journal.pbio.0050168.

Ostevik, Kate L., Jessamyn Manson, and James D.Thomson, "Pollination Potential of Male Bumble Bees (*Bombus impatiens*): Movement Patterns and Pollen-Transfer Efficiency." *Journal of Pollination Ecology* 2, no. 4 (2010): 21–26.

Palmier, Kirsten M., and Cory S. Sheffield. "First Records of the Common Eastern Bumble Bee, *Bombus impatiens* Cresson (Hymenoptera: Apidae, Apinae, Bombini) from the Prairies Ecozone on Canada." *Biodiversity Data Journal* 7 (2019): e30953. DOI: 10.3897/BDJ.7.e30953.

Peng, Gary, John C. Sutton, and Peter Kevan. "Effectiveness of Honey Bees for Applying the Biocontrol Agent *Gliocladium roseum* to Strawberry Flowers to Suppress *Botrytis cinerea*." *Canadian Journal of Plant Pathology* 14, no. 2 (1992): 117–188.

Perry, Clint J., Luigi Baciadonna, and Lars Chittka, "Unexpected Rewards Induce Dopamine-Dependent Positive Emotion-like State Changes in Bumblebees." *Science* 353, no. 6307 (2016): 1529–1531. DOI: 10.1126/science.aaf4454.

Plowright, C. M. S. "Bumblebees at Work in an Emotion-Like State." *Learning & Behavior* 45 (2017): 207–208. DOI: 10.3758/s13420-017-0265-2.

Prŷs-Jones, Oliver E., Kristján Kristjánsson, and Erling Ólafsson. "Hitchhiking with the Vikings? The Anthropogenic Bumble Bee Fauna of Iceland—Past and Present." *Journal of Natural History* 50, no. 45–46 (2016): 2895–2916.

Ratti, Claudia M., & Sheila R. Colla. "Discussion of the Presence of an Eastern Bumble Bee species (*Bombus impatiens* Cresson) in Western Canada." *Pan-Pacific Entomologist* 86, no. 2 (2010): 29–31. DOI: 10.3956/2009-19.1.

Reade, Carol, Robbin Thorp, Koichi Goka, Marius Wasbauer, and Mark McKenna. "Invisible Compromises: Global Business, Local Ecosystems, and the Commercial Bumble Bee Trade." *Organization & Environment* 28, no. 4 (2015): 436–457.

Reeh, K. W., Neil Kirk Hillier, and G. Christopher Cutler. "Potential of Bumble Bees as Bio-Vectors of *Clonostachys rosea* for Botrytis Blight Management in Lowbush Blueberry." *Journal of Pest Science* 87 (2014): 543–550.

Rundlöf, Maj, Georg K. S. Andersson, Riccardo Bommarco, Ingemar Fries, Veronica Hederström, Lina Herbertsson, Ove Jonsson, Björn K. Klatt, Thorsten R. Pedersen, Johanna Yourstone, and Henrik G. Smith. "Seed Coating with a Neonicotinoid Insecticide Negatively Affects Wild Bees." *Nature* 521 (2015): 77–80. DOI: 10.1038/nature14420.

Sachman-Ruiz, Bernardo, Verónica Narváez-Padilla, and Enrique Reynaud. "Commercial *Bombus impatiens* as Reservoirs of Emerging Infectious Diseases in Central México." *Biological Invasions* 17 (2015): 2043–2053. DOI: 10.1007/s10530-015-0859-6.

Sánchez-Bayo, Francisco, Dave Goulson, Francesco Pennacchio, Francesco Nazzi, Koichi Goka, and Nicolas Desneux. "Are Bee Diseases Linked to Pesticides? A Brief Review." *Environment International* 89–90 (2016): 7–11.

Schmid-Hempel, Regula, Michael Eckhardt, David Goulson, Daniel Heinzmann, Carlos Lange, Santiago Plischuk, Luisa R. Escudero, Rahel Salathé, Jessica J. Scriven, and Paul Schmid-Hempel. "The Invasion of Southern South America by Imported Bumble Bees and Associated Parasites." *Journal of Animal Ecology* 83 (2014): 823–837.

Sellars, Robin, and Barry Hicks. "Bee Diversity and Abundance in Three Different Habitats of Eastern Newfoundland." *Journal of the Acadian Entomological Society* 11 (2015): 9–14.

Semmens, T. D., E. Turner, and R. Buttermore. "*Bombus terrestris* (L.) (Hymenoptera: Apidae) Now Established in Tasmania." *Journal of the Australian Entomological Society* 32 (1993): 346.

Sharma, V. P., and Neelima R. Kumar. "Changes in Honey Bee Behaviour and Biology Under the Influence of Cell Phone Radiations." *Current Science* 98, no. 10 (2010): 1376–1378.

Shipp, Les, Jean Pierre Kapongo, Hong-Hyun Park, and Peter Kevan. "Effect of Bee-Vectored *Beauveria bassiana* on Greenhouse Beneficials under Greenhouse Cage Conditions." *Biological Control* 63 (2012): 135–142.

Stanley, Dara A., Avery L. Russell, Sarah J. Morrison, Catherine Rogers, and Nigel E. Raine. "Investigating the Impacts of Field-Realistic Exposure to a Neonicotinoid Pesticide on Bumblebee Foraging, Homing Ability and Colony Growth." *Journal of Applied Ecology* 53 (2016): 1440–1449. DOI: 10.1111/1365-2664.12689.

Stout, Jane C., & Dave Goulson. "Bumble Bees in Tasmania: Their Distribution and Potential Impact on Australian Flora and Fauna." *Bee World* 81, no. 2 (2000): 80–86.

Streit, Sebastian, Fiola Bock, Christian W. W. Pirk, and Jürgen Tautz. "Automatic Life-Long Monitoring of Individual Insect Behaviour Now Possible." *Zoology* 106, no. 3 (2003): 169–171.

Switzer, Callin M., Katja Hogendoorn, Sridhar Ravi, and Stacey A. Combes. "Shakers and Head bangers: Differences in Sonication Behavior Between

Australian *Amegilla murrayensis* (Blue-Banded Bees) and North American *Bombus impatiens* (Bumble Bees)." *Arthropod-Plant Interactions* 10 (2016): 1–8. DOI: 10.1007/s11829-015-9407-7.

Torretta, Juan P., Diego Medan, and Alberto H. Abrahamovich. "First Record of the Invasive Bumble Bee *Bombus terrestris* (L.) (Hymenoptera, Apidae) in Argentina." *Transactions of the American Entomological Society* 132, no. 3–4 (2006): 285–289.

Tsuchida, Koji, Ayumi Yamaguchi, Yuya Kanbe, and Koichi Goka. "Reproductive Interference in an Introduced Bumble Bee: Polyandry May Mitigate Negative Reproductive Impact." *Insects* 10, no. 2 (2019): 59 DOI: 10.3390/insects10020059.

Van Delm, Tom, S. Van Beneden, V. Mommaerts, Peter Melis, Katrijn Stoffels, Felix L. Wäckers, and W. Baets. "Control of *Botrytis cinerea* in Strawberries with *Gliocladium catenulatum* Vectored by Bumble Bees." *Journal of Berry Research* 5 (2015): 23–28.

vanEngelsdorp, Dennis, Jay D. Evans, Claude Saegerman, Chris Mullin, Eric Haubruge, Bach Kim Nguyen, et al. "Colony Collapse Disorder: A Descriptive Study." *PLoS ONE* 4, no. 8 (2009): e6481. DOI: 10.1371/journal.pone.0006481.

Velthuis, Hayo H. W., and Adriaan van Doorn. "A Century of Advances in Bumble Bee Domestication and the Economic and Environmental Aspects of its Commercialization for Pollination." *Apidologie* 37, no. 4 (2006): 421–451. DOI: 10.1051/apido:2006019.

Walker, C. M., and C. M. S. Plowright. "Single Bumblebee Leaving Colony for the First Time Seeks Company." *Behaviour* 152, no. 15 (2015): 2127–2143. DOI: 10.1163/1568539X-00003318.

Waters, Joe, Steph O'Connor, Kirsty J. Park, and Dave Goulson. "Testing a Detection Dog to Locate Bumblebee Colonies and Estimate Nest Density." *Apidologie* 42 (2011): 200–205.

Whittington, R., M. L. Winston, C. Tucker, and A. L. Parachnowitsch. "Plant-Species Identity of Pollen Collected by Bumble Bees Placed in Greenhouses for Tomato Pollination." *Canadian Journal of Plant Science* 84, no. 2 (2004): 599–602.

Williams, Paul H. "The Distribution of Bumble Bee Colour Patterns Worldwide: Possible Significance for Thermoregulation, Crypsis, and Warning Mimicry." *Biological Journal of the Linnean Society* 92, no.1 (2007): 97–118.

———. "The Distribution and Decline of British Bumble Bees (*Bombus* Latr)." *Journal of Apicultural Research* 21 no. 4 (1982): 236–245.

———. "Phylogenetic Relationships among Bumble Bees (*Bombus* Latr.): A Reappraisal of Morphological Evidence." *Systematic Entomology* 19, no. 4 (1994): 327–344.

Wood, Thomas James, and Dave Goulson. "The Environmental Risks of Neonicotinoid Pesticides: A Review of the Evidence Post 2013." *Environmental Science and Pollution Research* 24, no. 21 (2017): 17285–17325. DOI: 10.1007/s11356-017-9240-x.

Woodcock, B. A., J. M. Bullock, R. F. Shore, M. S. Heard, M. G. Pereira, J. Redhead, L. Ridding, H. Dean, D. Sleep, P. Henrys, J. Peyton, S. Hulmes, L. Hulmes, M. Sárospataki, C. Saure, M. Edwards, E. Genersch, S. Knäbe, and R. F. Pywell. "Country-Specific Effects of Neonicotinoid Pesticides on Honey Bees and Wild Bees." *Science* 356 (2017): 1393–1395.

Wu-Smart, Judy, and Marla Spivak. "Effects of Neonicotinoid Imidacloprid Exposure on Bumble Bee (Hymenoptera: Apidae) Queen Survival and Nest Initiation." *Environmental Entomology* 47, no. 1 (2018): 55–62. DOI: 10.1093/ee/nvx175.

Photo Credits

Acknowledgments

Just as a colony of bumble bees works together, a colony of talented and knowledgeable people is needed to create a book. There are a lot of busy worker bees for me to thank, who each played their own special role in bringing this book to life.

Lisa Sandell, whose vision and enthusiasm was the first spark to light the flame.

Stacey Kondla: amazing agent, cheerleader, and magic-maker extraordinaire!

Amanda Shih, whose editorial brilliance and gentle guidance really helped to make my words shine.

Dr. Henry Lickers, who so kindly and generously shared his people's knowledge with me, so that I could share it with readers.

All the scientists who answered my many questions about their research and/or all other things bumble bee: Dr. Marcelo Aizen, Dr. Sheila Colla, Dr. Elaine Evans, Dr. Dave Goulson, Rich Hatfield, Dr. Barry Hicks, Sarina Jepsen, Amanda Liczner, Jose Montalva, Dr. Carolina Morales, Dr. Steph O'Connor, Dr. Oliver Prŷs-Jones,

Genevieve Rowe, Dr. Cory Sheffield, Hayley Tompkins, Dr. Amy Toth, Dr. Koji Tsuchida, and Dr. Paul Williams.

Dr. Eduardo Zattara, for providing such spectacular photos of his work with Dr. Amy Toth on the giant ginger bumble bee.

Alice Whitelaw, at Working Dogs for Conservation, for allowing me to feature her hardworking dogs in this book.

Helen King, Arlette Sijmonsma, Miyuki Santiago, and Lise Verachtert, the Kitchener Public Library, the Ottawa Public Library, and the Waterloo Public Library, who all helped me forage for information.

Cia Penner, for her encouragement, keen eye, wisdom, wit, and eagerness to read the next chapter.

Sairah Naheed, for endless friendship and bee-book cupcakes.

Dr. Catherine Plowright, who is probably wondering, "Why are you thanking me?" To which I say, the time I spent as your student studying bumble bees all those years ago made a lifelong impression on me. You gave me the opportunity to fall in love with bumble bees, and you also helped me to learn that in the quest to understand the other creatures with whom we share this Earth, great things come in small packages.

And last, but most certainly not least, Stephen, Lelynd, and Lexi. Thank you for your love, your support, your silliness, and your patience while Momma worked on her book.

Index

Note: Page numbers in *italics* refer to illustrations or graphs.

About the Author

DANA CHURCH studied bumble bees for her PhD at the University of Ottawa, Canada. As a kid she loved making little books about science topics. This is her first published book. She lives in southern Ontario with her husband; their two children; and their big, black, friendly dog.

You can find out more about Dana and her writing at danachurchwriter.com.